THE COUNTRY K1

MW00973968

By

Bob Howell and Gwen Earnest Howell

©2011 Bob Howell and Gwen Earnest Howell

All Rights Reserved

History and Food of the Southern United States

The population of the Southern United States is made up of many different peoples who came to the region in a variety of ways, each contributing to what is now called "Southern cooking." American Indians, native to the region, taught European settlers to grow and cook corn, a grain unknown in Europe at the time. Spanish explorers in the 1500s brought pigs with them, introducing pork to the region. West Africans carried some of their traditional foods with them, such as watermelon, eggplant, collard greens, and okra, when they were brought to the United States by force as slaves beginning in the 1600s. Creoles, known for their unique use of spices, are descended from French and Haitian immigrants who later mingled with Spanish settlers in the New Orleans area. "Cajuns" also recognized for their unique style of cooking, were originally Acadians, French settlers in Nova Scotia who were driven out by the British in 1755 and made their way to New Orleans. In Louisiana, crawfish (resemble miniature lobsters) and catfish are popular, prepared in dozens of different ways. Fried catfish is popular all across the South. Texas's spicy and flavorful "Tex-Mex" cuisine reflects the state's close proximity to the spicy cuisine of Mexico.

The American Civil War (1861–1865) had a major impact on the South and its food. Many plantations and farms were destroyed during the conflict. To survive, Southerners ate whatever they could grow or find, and nothing went to waste. When the economy began to recover, most African Americans were not allowed to share in the newfound wealth and continued to eat the simple foods that were available during the war. This type of simple and inexpensive food became known later as "soul food." The first African American, and the only ex-slave, known to have written a cookbook was Abby Fisher. Her book, *What Mrs. Fisher Knows About Old Southern Cooking*, was published in 1881 and includes many recipes that would now be considered soul food.

Because kitchens only had wood-burning stoves in the late 1800s, recipes did not give baking temperatures or times. Bakers simply had to guess how long something would take to bake and keep checking it. Even if they had baked something many times before, the fire could be hotter or cooler each time, so baked goods had to be checked frequently to make sure they did not burn.

The staple food of the Southern United States is corn—it is used in grits (hulled and coarsely ground corn cooked to a thick—soup consistency and eaten at breakfast), a wide variety of breads and cakes, and as a breading on fried foods. Corn is native to the United States and was introduced to European settlers by American Indians. Another staple food in the South is pork, originally brought to America by Spanish explorers in the 1500s. Chitterlings (pronounced CHIT-lins), made from pig intestines, were traditionally seen as a "poor person's" food, but have recently begun to appear in fine restaurants. Barbecued meat, usually pork, on a grill is a Southern tradition.

Besides grits, most people also think of southern-fried chicken when they hear "Southern cooking." Traditionally served for Sunday dinner, fried chicken has become a stereotype of Southern food, popularized by Colonel Sanders' Kentucky Fried Chicken. Other meats, such as steak, are also "chicken-fried" in the South by breading and frying them. Cornbread, made from cornmeal, is typically eaten with a Southern meal.

Okra, black-eyed peas, and collard greens are all common Southern-grown vegetables that were brought to the region by African slaves. The name for meat stew, gumbo, often thickened with okra, comes from a West African word for okra, quingombo . Jambalaya, a pork and rice stew from the Creole and Cajun New Orleans region, takes its name from the French and Spanish words for ham: jambon and jamón , respectively. Crawfish, catfish, and shrimp are enjoyed all across the South.

Favorite desserts in the South include chess pie, sweet potato pie, pecan pie, key lime pie, and watermelon, which is also the most popular melon in the United States.

Most US Southerners are Christian, for whom the main holidays are Christmas and Easter. It is a longstanding tradition in the South to make fruitcake for Christmas. The Claxton Fruitcake Company in Georgia sells more than 200 tons of fruitcake each year. The typical main dish for both holidays is ham. Southerners are known for their country ham, a hindquarter of a year-old hog that is preserved with either salt or sugar, smoked, and then aged for a year or more.

Another Christian holiday that receives special treatment in the South is Mardi Gras (French for "Fat Tuesday"), the day of feasting before Lent begins. New Orleans is famous for its Mardi Gras celebration, which lasts several days and involves parades, balls, music, and lots of food. One traditional element of the feast is the King Cake in which a small figurine or dried bean is baked inside. Whoever gets the piece with the figurine in it is crowned king or queen for the day.

 The main meal of the day in the Southern United States used to be at midday and was called "dinner." The smaller evening meal was referred to as "supper." In recent years, the main meal has moved to the evening, though most Southerners still call it "dinner." During the 1800s, the era of large plantations, guests would often come to visit for days or weeks at a time. Hospitality is very important to Southerners, and hosts prepare huge meals for their guests. A dinner menu from the mid-1800s may have included five kinds of meat, cucumbers and tomatoes, hot rolls, and five different desserts, plus three beverages. The African slaves did not share in this abundance of food, but lived on small amounts of salt pork, cornbread, and hominy (corn mush), plus whatever greens they could grow themselves.

 This meager diet became the basis for what is known today as "soul food."

Southerners' favorite beverages are iced tea, usually loaded with sugar and called "sweet tea," and soft drinks, many of which were invented in the South. Coca-Cola was developed in 1886 in Atlanta, Georgia. Pepsi was created 10 years later in North Carolina. Dr. Pepper first appeared in Waco, Texas, in 1885, and Mountain Dew was first produced in either Virginia or Tennessee around 1961. Other Southern-made soft drinks include Royal Crown Cola, Nehi fruit-flavored drinks, Barq's root beer, and Gatorade. The South continues to be the largest consumer, as well as producer, of soft drinks. In the 1990s, North Carolina was the number one soft-drink consumer of the 50 states with over 50 gallons consumed per person per year.

Other snack foods native to the South include corn dogs (hot dogs breaded with cornmeal), pralines (almond or pecan clusters), and the Moon Pie (a chocolate-coated marshmallow sandwich cookie), invented at the Chattanooga Bakery in Tennessee in 1917.

People living in the Southern states generally receive adequate nutrition in their diets. Traditional Southern cooking is high in fat and calories, and many modern Southerners are striving for a healthier lifestyle, reserving the delicious fried and sugary foods for special occasions and celebrations.

Southern teens and adults are slightly more likely than people from other parts of the United States to smoke cigarettes. This is due in part to the role tobacco farming has played in the economies of such states as Kentucky, Tennessee, Virginia, and North and South Carolina.

Table of Contents

Appetizers & Beverages

Candy Bar Frosties

1	can	Eagle Brand Milk	2 or 3		candy bars broken
1	8-oz ctn	plain or vanilla yogurt	2	cups	ice crushed
½	cup	Chocolate Flavor Syrup			

In blender container, combine Eagle Brand and other remaining ingredients; blend until smooth. Serve immediately. Garnish as desired. Refrigerate or freeze leftovers.

Cheese Ball

1	cup	sharp cheddar cheese, grated	1	Tbsp	red pepper
1	cup	pepper jack cheese, grated	1	Tbsp	Tabasco sauce
1	block	cream cheese, softened	1	cup	pecan pieces

Put all ingredients in a bowl and mix together. Shape into ball and roll in pecan pieces. Cover with wrap. Serve with crackers

Cheese Ball

2	cups	cheese grated	½	tsp	garlic powder
1	8-ounce	cream cheese, softened	1	tsp	Worcestershire sauce
½	cup	pecans, chopped	1	tsp	red pepper

Blend cream cheese, grated cheese and seasonings. Shape into ball and roll in nuts. Serve with crackers

Cheese Rolls

1	pkg	cream cheese, softened	¼	tsp	worcestershire sauce
1	lb	cheddar cheese shredded			Paprika, to taste
¾	cup	walnut pieces			

Beat cream cheese until smooth. Blend in cheddar cheese. Stir in walnuts and worcestershire sauce. Divide mixture into thirds. Shape each section into a log. Roll in paprika. Wrap in saran wrap and chill at least 3 hours. Serve thin slices on crackers

Cream Cheese Crab Spread

1	can	cream of mushroom soup	1	Tbs	hot sauce
1	8-ounce	cream cheese, softened	1	6 to 8-ounce	imitation crabmeat
1	cup	mayonnaise	1	cup	celery chopped
½	tsp	lemon juice	½	cup	green onion chopped

Combine soup and cream cheese. Beat on low until mixed. Stir in mayonnaise, lemon juice and hot sauce. Fold in crabmeat, celery and onions.. Cover and chill for several hours. Serve on crackers or vegetable sticks

Cucumber Supreme

1	cup	white chicken cooked			salt, to taste
1		boiled egg chopped			pepper, to taste
¾	cup	mayonnaise	3	Tbs	pecans, toasted and chopped
¼	cup	celery chopped	5	doz	cucumber slices

Combine chicken, egg, mayonnaise, celery, salt, pepper and nuts. Refrigerate 2 hours. Spread 1 tsp of chicken mixture on each cucumber slice. Top with additional chopped nuts if desired

Dandelion Wine

1	gallon	dandelion blossoms	3	lbs	sugar
1	gallon	boiling water			orange and lemon pulp with juices
2		lemon rinds finely grated	½	cake	yeast
2		orange rinds finely grated			

Pour 1 gallon of boiling water over 1 gallon of dandelion blossoms and let stand in a cool place for 72 hours. Pour the liquid in a kettle and add the rind of 2 lemons and 2 oranges (grated fine) and boil for ½ hour. Add three pounds of sugar and the pulp and juices of the fruit and allow the mixture to cool, then add a ½ yeast cake. Strain through a fine cloth and allow the liquid to stand for 1 week in a warm place. Repeat straining process to assure the liquid is clear. When it stops fermenting bottle the wine. Pick early in the season when the leaves of the plant are still tender. Flowers that have just opened are best for Dandelion wine.

Dressed Potato Chips

1	pkg	ranch dressing	¼	tsp	lemon pepper
¾	cup	oil	½	tsp	garlic
¼	tsp	dill weed			

Mix dry ingredients then add oil. Stir and pour over potato chips. Bake at 275° for 15 to 20 minutes

Eggnog

4 ½	cups	milk	4	tsp	brandy or rum extract
¼	cup	sugar	¼	tsp	salt
6		eggs, separated			nutmeg
1	pint	vanilla ice cream			

Combine milk and ¼ cup sugar in a saucepan. Heat over medium heat stirring to dissolve sugar until a rim of bubbles forms. Beat egg yolks until thick and lemon colored. Add small amount of the hot milk to egg yolks then add to milk mixture. Cook over medium heat for 5 minutes. Pour into bowl. Add ice cream by spoonfuls stirring until melted. Add extract. Cover and refrigerate. Refrigerate egg whites. Before serving bring egg whites to room temperature. Beat egg whites until foamy. Add salt and beat to soft peak. Gently fold into eggnog. Top with nutmeg and serve

Elderberry Wine

| 3 | lbs | elderberries | 1 | | lemon |
| 3 | lbs | sugar | ½ | oz | yeast |

To remove the berries from the stalks, use a fork. Put berries in a sanitized bucket and pour on gallon of boiling water. Mash the berries against the side of the bucket. Cover and leave for 3 or 4 days. Strain and tip the liquid back into bucket; add the sugar and stir until dissolved. Squeeze the lemon and add all the juice (to get the most juice from your lemon, cut it in half and put in microwave for 30 seconds). Sprinkle on the yeast. Cover for 3 days, strain again and pour wine into demijohn. Fix airlock and leave until bubbling completely stops (I left mine for about 5 months). Strain and bottle off. The wine could be ready to drink in about 4 months (if too young leave it for much longer). Has a lovely red color.

Fruit Frostie

| 2 | cups | fresh fruit of choice | 2 | cups | ice crushed |
| 1 | 8-oz ctn | plain or vanilla yogurt | | | |

In blender container, combine Eagle Brand and other remaining ingredients; blend until smooth. Serve immediately. Garnish as desired. Refrigerate or freeze leftovers.

Holiday Punch

1	lg	orange Jello	2	lg	frozen lemonade
1	lg	strawberry Jello	1	lg	white grape juice
2	lg cans	orange juice	1	quart	boiling water
2	cups	sugar	2	quarts	cold water
2	lg cans	pineapple juice			Ginger Ale

Use large pot to mix punch. Dissolve jello and sugar in boiling water. Add all other ingredients. Pour into jugs until 3/4 full. Freeze until ready to use. Add 1 pint Ginger Ale to each gallon punch before serving.

Horse Back Angels

1	pint	oysters	12	slices	bacon
1	tsp	salt	½	tsp	pepper
½	tsp	paprika			

Drain oysters and put on top of a half piece bacon. Sprinkle seasonings on top. Wrap bacon around oyster and fasten with toothpick. Place in baking dish and bake at 450° until bacon is crisp.

Luscious Slush Punch

2½	cups	sugar	1	46 oz can	pineapple juice
6	cups	water	2/3	cup	lemon juice
2	3-ounce boxes	strawberry gelatin	2	2 liter bottles	lemon-lime drink

In a large saucepan, combine sugar, water, and strawberry flavored gelatin. Boil for 3 minutes. Stir in pineapple juice, lemon juice, and orange juice. Divide mixture in half, and freeze in 2 separate containers. When ready to serve, place the frozen contents of one container in a punch bowl, and stir in 1 bottle of lemon-lime soda until slushy.

Mulled Cider

2	quarts	sweet cider		mace	
3	sticks	cinnamon	2	cups	brown sugar
		cloves	1	cup	spiced crab apples
		allspice			

Put 2 quarts of sweet cider in a kettle, add 3 sticks of cinnamon and allow the liquid to simmer Tie cloves, allspice and mace in a cloth bag and drop into the boiling cider. Stir in 2 cups of brown sugar, beat slowly and add 1 cup spiced crab apples. Serve hot with 1 apple in each cup.

Refrigerator Tea

4	tea bags, family sized	1	cup	lemon juice
3	mint springs	1 ½	cups	sugar
½ can	orange juice, frozen			

Steep tea bags and mint in boiling water for 10 minutes. Strain into gallon container. Add remaining ingredients and enough water to make full gallon. Refrigerate and stir before serving.

Rhubarb Punch

4	cups	rhubarb	¼ cup	lemon juice
2	cups	sugar		ginger ale
½	cup	orange juice		

Skin and cut into small pieces 4 cups of rhubarb and boil until soft in 1 quart of water. Strain through a cloth, add 2 cups of sugar and bring to a boil. Add ½ cup of orange juice, ¼ cup of lemon juice and chill. Serve in equal amounts of ginger ale over ice.

Sausage Cheese Balls

1 ½	cups	Biscuit Mix	8 oz		hot sausage
8 oz		sharp cheddar cheese, grated			

Preheat oven to 350°. Combine biscuit mix, sausage and cheese. Knead in large bowl. Roll into small balls. Bake for 12 to 15 minutes or until brown on ungreased pan. Drain on paper towels when done.

Spicy Pineapple Chunks

1	can (15 oz)	pineapple chunks, drained	1 ¼	cups	sugar
¾	cup	vinegar			salt (dash)
1		cinnamon stick	6 to 8		cloves

Add all ingredients in a boiler; bring to boil. Remove from heat and refrigerate until serving time. Drain well. Serve ice cold with wooden picks.

Stuffed Mushrooms

½	lb	mushrooms	6	slices	bacon
1	8-ounce	cream cheese, softened			garlic salt, to taste

Rinse mushrooms then break off stems. Fry bacon until crisp then crumble. Mix bacon with cream cheese. Add garlic salt. Scoop cheese mixture into mushrooms. Bake at 350° on lightly greased cookie sheet until cheese is light brown.

Sugared Peanuts

4	cups	pecans	2	cups	sugar
1	cup	water	¼	tsp	salt
½	tsp	vanilla			

Boil sugar and water until it begins to "sugar" on sides. Add rest of the ingredients and cook until all the water is cooked out. Spread on a cookie sheet and bake at 225° for 40 minutes. Stir once or twice while baking

Sweet Tea

5		family sized tea bags	2	cups	boiling water
1 ½	cups	sugar			cold water
¼	tsp	baking soda			

Bring water to a boil then add tea bags and soda. Cover and steep for 15 minutes. Remove tea bags then pour into gallon tea pitcher. Add sugar and stir until dissolved. Fill with cold water and stir again. Refrigerate until cold.

Watermelon Lemonade

8	cups	watermelon seeded and cut in chunks	½		fresh lemon juice
1	quart	strawberries hulled and quartered	2	cups	water
1	cup	sugar			

In a food processor fitted with a steel blade, pulse the watermelon, strawberries, and sugar until blended and smooth. Strain through a fine-mesh strainer into a 2-quart container, pushing down on the solids to get all the juice. Add the lemon juice and enough of the water to make 1 1/2 quarts. Chill until very cold. Serve over ice with a wedge of watermelon

Breads & Rolls

Banana Bread

1	cup	walnuts or pecans, toasted and coarsely chopped (optional)	1/4	tsp	salt
1 3/4	cups	all-purpose flour	1	tsp	ground cinnamon
3/4	cup	granulated white sugar	2	lg	eggs, lightly beaten
1	tsp	baking powder	1/2	cup	unsalted butter, melted and cooled
1/4	tsp	baking soda	3	lg	ripe bananas, mashed well (about 1-1/2 cups)
			1	tsp	pure vanilla extract

Preheat oven to 350° and place oven rack to middle position. Butter and flour (or spray with a non stick vegetable/flour spray) the bottom and sides of a 9 x 5 x 3 inch loaf pan. Set aside.

Place the nuts on a baking sheet and bake for about 8 to 10 minutes or until lightly toasted. Let cool and then chop coarsely.

In a large bowl combine the flour, sugar, baking powder, baking soda, salt, cinnamon, and nuts. Set aside.

In a medium-sized bowl combine the mashed bananas, eggs, melted butter, and vanilla. With a rubber spatula or wooden spoon, lightly fold the wet ingredients (banana mixture) into the dry ingredients just until combined and the batter is thick and chunky. (The important thing is not to over mix the batter. You do not want it smooth. Over mixing the batter will yield tough, rubbery bread.) Scrape batter into prepared pan. Bake until bread is golden brown and a toothpick inserted in the center comes out clean, about 55 to 60 minutes. Place on a wire rack to cool and then remove the bread from the pan. Serve warm or at room temperature. This bread can be frozen.

Banana Bread

2	cups	self rising flour	½	cup	butter
1	cup	sugar	1	cup	nuts, chopped
2		eggs		dash	salt
3		bananas, mashed			

Cream butter and sugar. Add bananas, eggs and flour. Mix all ingredients. Bake at 325° in a greased loaf pan for 1 hour (or until knife comes out clean)

Beer Bread

3	cups	self rising flour	1	12 oz can	warm beer
3	tbl	sugar			

Mix all ingredients in a glass bowl. Put into a greased bread pan. Let rise about 15 minutes. Bake at 400° for 30 minutes or until brown.

Biscuits

4	cups	self rising flour	¼ cup	oil
1	cup	buttermilk		

Make a well in the flour and add buttermilk and oil. Squish together picking up flour. As the mixture get thicker begin lifting toward the center in a circular motion. Press down on the center with each lift. When a dough is formed choke biscuits and place on greased baking pan. Bake at 375° for 20 minutes or until golden brown

Blueberry Muffins

1¾	cups	self rising flour	¾ cup	milk
½	cup	sugar	1	egg
1	cup	blueberries, fresh or thawed frozen	½ cup	butter, melted

Combine flour and sugar. Stir in berries. Add milk, eggs and butter. Mix until moistened. Batter will be lumpy. Spoon into greased muffin cups. Bake at 400° for 25 minutes or tops spring back when touched.

Can substitute other berries in place of blueberries

Bob's Fried Cornbread

1	cup	plain cornmeal	1 tsp	salt
1	tbl	mayonnaise		hot water

Mix cornmeal, salt and mayonnaise with hot water until it is thick pancake batter consistency. Drop by spoonfuls into hot grease. fry until golden brown. Drain on paper towels. Best cooked in an iron fryer

Coffee Can Bread

4	cups	all purpose flour, divided	¼ cup	sugar
1	pkg	yeast	1 tsp	salt
½	cup	milk	2	eggs
½	cup	water		

Mix 2 cups flour with dry yeast. In a saucepan, combine milk, water, butter, sugar and salt. Cook over low heat until butter melts. Stir constantly to avoid sticking. Cool for 5 minutes then add to flour and yeast mixture. Add eggs and remaining flour alternately to make soft dough. Knead on floured surface about 5 minutes. Divide into 2 parts and shape into balls. Grease two 1 lb coffee cans. Place dough balls in each of the cans. Place in warm area and let rise until it is about an inch from the top of can. Bake at 375° for 30 minutes or until brown. Can substitute 2 loaf pans if coffee cans are not available

Corn Dodgers

1½	cups	self rising corn meal mix	1	tsp	salt
4	tbl	flour	1	cup	hot water

Combine meal, flour and salt. Add water to make a stiff mixture. Make balls and drop into greens as they cook. Cook for 30 minutes. Mixture must be stiff or the corn dodgers will come apart

Cornbread

2	cups	self rising corn meal	2	cups	buttermilk
3		eggs	¼	cup	shortening

Melt shortening in iron skillet while preheating oven. Mix milk and egg with self rising corn meal. Pour melted shortening into batter and mix. Pour into cast iron skillet and bake at 400° until browned

Cracklin Bread

1 3/4	cup	cornmeal mix	2	cup	buttermilk
2		eggs, beaten	1	cup	cracklings or pork rinds

Combine cornmeal, flour, baking powder, and soda. Mix well. Add eggs, buttermilk and cracklings, stirring well. Heat a well greased cast iron skillet in 400° oven for 3 minutes. Pour batter into hot skillet. Bake at 400° for 35 minutes or until golden brown.

Egg Bread

6		eggs	1½	cups	buttermilk
2	cups	corn meal mix	¼	cup	oil

Mix together. Add more buttermilk if it is too thick. Place in oiled iron skillet that has been preheated to 350°. Bake for 20 minutes or until golden brown

Friendship Bread

1	pkg	active dry yeast	2	cups	sifted flour
1/2	cup	warm water	1	tsp	salt
1 1/2	cups	lukewarm water			

Dissolve yeast in 1/2 cup warm water. Stir in 1 1/2 cups water, flour, salt, and sugar. Beat until smooth. Let stand uncovered at room temperature three to five days stirring 2 or 3 times a day. Use a wooden spoon. Cover at night.

When the mixture is ready it should have a yeasty smell. Then pour out one cup of this to use in the friendship mixture. The rest should stand one day and then be refrigerated covered. Use within 10 days. Now, with the 1 cup you took out, add 1/2 cup water, 1/2 cup flour and 1 teaspoon sugar. Consider this day one and follow Amish Bread Recipe.

Do not use metal spoon. Do not refrigerate. The day you receive the started mixture - do nothing. Days 2, 3, and 4 stir with a wooden spoon. Day five add 1 cup flour, 1 cup sugar and 1 cup milk. STIR. Days 6, 7, 8, and 9 only stir the mixture. Day 10 add 1 cup flour, 1 cup sugar, one cup milk and stir. Pour 1 cup mixture into each of the three separate containers and give to three friends.

The remaining mixture add 2/3 cup oil, 3 eggs, 2 cups flour, 1 cup sugar, 1 teaspoon cinnamon, 1 1/2 teaspoon baking powder, 1/2 teaspoon baking soda and 1/2 teaspoon salt. Add fruits, nuts, raisins or chopped apple. Before baking, pour into 2 well greased and sugared loaf pans. Bake 45 to 50 minutes at 350°. Cool 10 minutes.

Golden Muffins

2	cups	self rising flour	2		eggs well beaten
2	tbl	sugar	1	cup	milk
4	tbl	lard			

Mix flour, sugar and lard. Add eggs and milk and beat carefully. Bake in a greased muffin pan on medium heat until golden brown.

Good Bread

Dissolve 2 cakes of yeast, add 5 pounds of flour, 1 ounce of salt, 1 ½ ounces of sugar, two ounces of lard, ½ cup of milk, ½ cup of luke-warm water.

Mix and kneed carefully. Let the dough rise for several hours, punch the mixture back and kneed and let it rise again for 45 minutes. Puncture again and let it rise for 15 minutes. Place dough in pans and let it rise for 1 hour then bake for 45 minutes.

NOTE: keep the dough at around 80 degrees until baking.

Hush Puppies

2	cups	self rising corn meal mix	1	tsp	garlic powder
1		egg beaten	½	small	onion finely chopped
1	cup	buttermilk			

Mix all ingredients to make a stiff batter. Shape into balls and drop into deep fat heated to 375°. Fry until golden brown. Hushpuppies will roll over when touched when ready to turn

Jo Linda's Rolls

5	cups	self rising flour	¾	cup	cooking oil
1	tbl	sugar	1	pkg	yeast
1	tsp	soda	¼	cup	warm water
2	cups	buttermilk			

Mix well all ingredients except yeast and water. Dissolve yeast in warm water and mix with other ingredients. Let set 2 hours. Cover and keep in refrigerator. When ready to bake pinch into rolls and bake at 350° until brown

Mayonnaise Rolls

1	cup	self rising flour	1	tbl	mayonnaise
½	cup	milk			

Mix milk and mayonnaise then stir in flour. Mix and pour into 6 oiled muffin tins. Bake at 450° until brown

Mexican Cornbread

1	lb	ground beef	1	can	creamed corn
½	lb	cheddar cheese grated	2		eggs well beaten
1	lg	onion chopped	¼	cup	cooking oil
1	sm can	green chili peppers	½	tsp	salt
1	cup	yellow cornmeal	1	tsp	soda
1	cup	milk			

Brown meat, onions and peppers and drain. Remove from heat and add cheese. Stir until cheese melts. Set aside. Mix meal, milk corn, eggs, oil, salt and soda. Put ½ of this mixture in greased iron skillet. Add meat mixture. Top with remaining bread mixture. Bake at 350° for 45 minutes or until brown.

Oatmeal Muffins

2	cups	self rising flour	2		eggs
2	cups	quick oats, uncooked	2	cups	buttermilk
1	cup	brown sugar firmly packed	¾	cup	shortening, melted
2	tsp	cinnamon			

Combine dry ingredients in large bowl and mix well. Stir together eggs, buttermilk and shortening. Add to dry ingredients stirring just until moistened. Spoon into greased muffin pans. Bake at 400° for 18 to 20 minutes

Old Timey Butter Rolls

2	cups	self rising flour	**Milk Sauce**		
½	cup	shortening	2	cups	milk
½	cup	milk	¾	cup	sugar
1	stick	butter	1	tsp	vanilla
¼	cup	sugar			
1	tsp	cinnamon			

Cut shortening into flour really well with a fork. Stir in milk. On a floured surface, dump out dough and press together with your hands to form a ball. Roll out into a rectangle (about 7×10 in size). Spread softened butter over dough and then sprinkle 1/4 cup sugar and cinnamon over top. Roll it up like a jelly roll and press it together lightly. Cut into nine slices about one inch thick each. Place into a lightly greased 8×8 baking dish. In medium sauce pot, combine all milk sauce ingredients. Heat over medium heat, stirring constantly, until mixture begins to bubble lightly. Pour over rolls in pan. Bake at 350° for 30-40 minutes, or until rolls are lightly browned on top. Allow to sit for a few minutes once it is done for the rolls to soak up more sauce. After you put each roll on a plate, spoon more sauce over it.

Parmesan Scallion Pinwheels

1		sheet frozen puff pastry, thawed	1/4	cup	grated parmesan
1	lg	egg, beaten	2	tbl	grated parmesan
3		scallions, thinly sliced			kosher salt and black pepper

Heat oven to 400°. Line a baking sheet with parchment. Unfold the pastry and brush with the egg. Sprinkle with the scallions, ¼ cup of the Parmesan, ¼ teaspoon salt, and ⅛ teaspoon pepper. Roll tightly into a log. Freeze until firm but still sliceable, about 20 minutes.

Slice the log into ¼-inch-thick rounds and place on the prepared baking sheet. Sprinkle with the remaining 2 tablespoons of Parmesan and bake until golden brown, 12 to 15 minutes. Serve warm or at room temperature.

Pumpkin Bread

3	cups	sugar	1	tsp	nutmeg
4		eggs	2/3	cup	water
1	cup	oil	2	cups	pumpkin
1½	tsp	salt	3½	cups	self rising flour
1	tsp	cinnamon			pecans and raisins optional

Mix all ingredients and pour into greased loaf pans. Bake at 350° for 1 hour or until knife comes out clean

Raisin Bran Loaf

1	cup	sugar	1	cup	raisins
3	cups	self rising flour	½	cup	walnuts, roughly chopped
2	cups	bran cereal	2	cups	buttermilk

Sift sugar and flour. Add cereal, nuts and raisins. Stir in buttermilk. Bake at 300° for 1 hour (or until knife comes out clean) in 2 greased loaf pans

Steamed Brown Bread

Combine 2 tbl of butter, ½ cup brown sugar, 2 eggs, 1 ½ cups of sour milk, 2 ½ tsp soda, ½ cup of dark molasses, 1 cup of white flour, 3 cups of bran, 1 cup of raisins, 1/3 cup of nut meats and 1 tsp salt.

Place the batter in tin cans, but leave at least an inch of space at the top. Steam the mixture for 1 ½ hours.

Desserts

Banana Pudding Cake

Kecia Howell Gilley

Cake

1	box	spice cake mix
1½	cups	water
1/3	cup	oil
3		eggs
1	tsp	vanilla butter and nut flavoring
½	cup	banana, peeled and mashed

Topping

1	cup	whipping cream, cold
1/3	cup	powdered sugar
1	tsp	vanilla
1	4 oz pkg	cream cheese, softened
1	pkg	instant vanilla pudding and pie mix
1¼	cups	milk, divided
½		nutmeg
1		banana, ripe

Preheat oven to 350. Coat 2 (8-inch) square cake pans with nonstick cooking spray. Combine cake mix, water, oil, eggs, and flavoring in medium bowl; beat with electric mixer at medium speed until blended. Mix in mashed banana. Pour into prepared pans. Bake 30 minutes or until toothpick inserted into centers comes out clean. Cool 15 minutes in pans on wire racks. Transfer to wire racks to cool completely. Beat whipping cream with electric mixer at high speed 1 1/2 to 2 minutes or until soft peaks form. Add powdered sugar and vanilla; beat 15 seconds or until stiff peaks form. Beat cream cheese, pudding mix and 1/4 cup milk in large bowl with electric mixer at low speed until well blended. Add remaining 1 cup milk and nutmeg. Increase speed to medium; beat until smooth. Fold in whipped cream. Cover with plastic wrap; refrigerate until needed to frost. Spread 3/4 cup pudding mixture evenly over top of one cake layer. Peel, slice and arrange banana evenly over cake. Top with second cake layer; frost with remaining pudding mixture. Refrigerate leftovers.

Bigmama's Chocolate Icing

½	cup	cocoa	½	stick	butter (no substitutes)
2	cups	sugar			evaporated milk, enough to dissolve sugar

Mix sugar and cocoa. Add canned milk slowly until mixture is dissolved. Add butter. Cook over low to medium heat stirring constantly until it comes to a rolling boil. Do not over cook as it will cause it to harden. Spread quickly over layers

Buttercream Frosting

1	lb	powdered sugar	1	tsp	vanilla
½	cup	butter (no substitutes)	3	tbl	milk

In a large bowl, beat together sugar, butter, vanilla and milk until smooth. If necessary, add more milk until has spreading consistency.

To make Chocolate Buttercream Frosting: melt 2 squares (1- ounce each) unsweetened chocolate over very low heat until melted. Stir into buttercream frosting.

Carrot Cake

2	cups	sugar		1	tsp	salt
2	cups	flour		1½	cups	oil
2	tsp	baking soda		4		eggs
2	tsp	cinnamon		3	cups	carrots, grated

Combine dry ingredients. Add eggs and oil, mixing well. Add carrots and beat on medium speed for 2 minutes. Pour into 3 greased and floured cake pans. Bake at 350° for 30 to 35 minutes or cake springs back when touched. Frost with Cream Cheese Icing

Chocolate Buttermilk Sheet Cake

2	cups	sugar		**Icing**		
2	cups	flour		1	stick	butter
2		eggs		6	tbl	buttermilk
½	cup	buttermilk		5	tbl	cocoa
1	tsp	baking soda		1	box	10 X sugar
				1	tsp	vanilla
				1	cup	nuts, chopped

Mix sugar and flour then add eggs, buttermilk and soda. Pour into greased and floured sheet pan. Bake at 300° until cake springs back when touched. When cake is nearly done begin the icing. Bring butter, buttermilk and cocoa to a boil. Remove from heat and add 10 X sugar, vanilla and chopped nuts. Stir well and pour over hot cake. Cool. Cut in squares

Cinnamon Nut Squares

1	cup	butter, softened		2	cups	self rising flour
½	cup	dark brown sugar, packed		1	tbl	cinnamon
½	cup	sugar		1½	cup	pecans, chopped
1	lg	egg separated				

Preheat oven to 300°. Cream sugars, butter and egg yolk until light and fluffy. Combine flour,and cinnamon. Add to beaten mixture and beat until blended. Pour into ungreased baking pan. Beat egg white until just foamy. Spread over dough. Sprinkle with nuts and press lightly. Bake for 40 minutes. Cut into squares while hot.

Country Cruellers

2		eggs		1	cup	sugar

1	tsp	nutmeg	1 tsp	baking soda
1	pint	milk	½ tsp	cream of tarter
8	tbl	butter		flour

Mix together eggs, nutmeg, pint of milk, butter, sugar, soda and cream of tarter. Add enough flour to roll. Cut dough into strips four inches long and place in hot oil. Remove when golden brown and sprinkle with powdered sugar

Cream Cheese Frosting

2	8 oz pkg	cream cheese, softened	2½ cups	10 X sugar sifted
1	stick	butter, unsalted, softened	pinch	salt
1	tsp	vanilla		

With an electric mixer, blend together cream cheese and butter until smooth. Turn mixer to low speed and blend in powdered sugar, salt and vanilla extract. Turn mixer on high and beat until light and fluffy. Use immediately or refrigerate, covered, until ready to use. If refrigerated, the frosting will need to be brought to room temperature before using (after frosting softens up, beat with mixer until smooth).

Cream Cheese Pound Cake

2	sticks	butter	6	eggs
1	8 oz pkg	cream cheese	3 cups	cake flour (not self-rising)
3	cups	sugar	1 tsp	vanilla

Cream butter, sugar and cream cheese together. Add remaining ingredients in order listed. Add eggs one at a time beating well after each addition. Pour into greased and floured tube pan and bake at 350° for 1½ hours

Creamy Frosting

1	box	instant pudding and pie filling your choice of flavor	1 cup	cold milk
¼	cup	confectioner's sugar	1 ctn	frozen whipped topping

Combine pudding mix, sugar and milk in a small bowl. Beat slowly with rotary beater or at lowest speed of electric mixer until well blended. Fold in whip topping and spread at once.

Easy Nut Cake

1	box	butter flavored cake mix	1 8 oz pkg	cream cheese
1	stick	butter	1 box	10 X sugar
3		eggs	1 cup	pecans, chopped

Mix cake mix, butter and 1 egg. Press into cake pan. Mix cream cheese, 2 eggs and 10X sugar and pour over cake. Press chopped nuts into cake. Bake at 350° for 45 minutes to 1 hour

Fresh Apple Cake

1	stick	butter	1	tsp	baking soda	
2	cups	sugar	1	tsp	salt	
2		eggs beaten	1½	cups	nuts, chopped	
2	cups	flour	1½	cups	dates, chopped	
1	tsp	cinnamon	4	cups	apples, peeled, cored and finely chopped	

Cream together butter and sugar. Add eggs. Mix well. Sift together flour and cinnamon. Add to cream mixture and mix well. Stir in nuts, dates and apples. Pour into well greased and floured tube pan. Bake 1 hour at 325° or bake in 2 loafs. Top with glaze

Fruit Fritters

1	cup	flour	1		egg beaten
1¼	tsp	baking powder	1/3	cup	milk
1	tsp	salt	1 to 2	cups	peach or apple filling drained
2	tbl	butter, melted			

Sift flour, baking powder, salt, and sugar into a large bowl. Combine egg, milk and melted butter, add to dry ingredients. Stir in fruit. Drop from large tablespoon onto non-stick grill. Fry slowly until golden brown.

Funnel Cakes

1	pint	milk	½	tsp	baking powder
2		eggs beaten			flour (enough to make loose batter)
	pinch	salt			

Combine milk, eggs, salt and baking powder with just enough flour to make a loose batter. Heat oil, enough to cover about one inch of dough. Pour batter through a funnel beginning in the center gradually pouring to the outward in a circular manner. (Do not allow the dough to tangle the previously poured batter). When the funnel cakes are light brown, remove from skillet and serve with maple syrup, a tart jelly or sprinkle them with powdered sugar

Glaze

½	stick	butter	1½	tsp	vanilla
2	cups	powdered sugar	3	tbl	water

Melt butter in a saucepan. Stir in powdered sugar and vanilla. Add water, 1 tablespoon at a time, and mix until smooth and of desired consistency (a thick syrup). Drizzle over cooled cake. (This will glaze one 12-cup bundt cake or a 10-inch angel food cake.)

Graham Cracker Squares

2	cups	graham cracker crumbs	1	cup	pecans, chopped
1	can	Eagle Brand Milk	1	sm pkg	chocolate chips

Mix together and pour into greased baking dish. Bake at 350° for 30 minutes. Cut into squares

Icebox Coconut Cake

1	box	yellow cake mix (butter recipe)	**Icing**		
4		eggs	1	cup	sour cream
1	cup	milk	2	cups	sugar
½	cup	oil	3	pkgs	frozen grated coconut

Mix cake mix, eggs, milk and oil. Beat until smooth. Bake in 4 greased and floured cake pans at 350° until cake springs back.

While cake is baking mix sour cream, sugar and coconut together. Frost layers while hot. Keep refrigerated

Lane Cake

Layers			½	tbl	Corn Syrup
2	sticks	butter (no substitutes), softened		dash	salt
2	cups	sugar	½	tsp	vanilla
3 ¼	cups	all purpose flour	**Filling**		
1	tbl	baking powder	8		egg yolks
¾	tsp	salt	1 ½	cups	sugar
1	cup	milk	1	stick	butter (no substitutes)
1	tsp	vanilla	1	cup	pecans
		egg whites, stiffly beaten reserving yolks	1	cup	raisins
			1	cup	coconut
Frosting			½	cup	sliced cherries
¾	cup	sugar	¼ to ½	cup	bourbon
3	tbl	water			
1		egg white			

Cream butter. Gradually add sugar. Beat well. Combine dry ingredients. Add to creamed mixture alternately with milk beginning and ending with flour mixture. Mix well after each addition. Stir in vanilla. FOLD in egg whites. Bake in 3 greased pans at 325° for 25 minutes or done when toothpick comes out clean.

Combine egg yolks, sugar and butter in a 2 quart saucepan. Cook over medium heat stirring constantly until thick. Remove from heat and stir in remaining ingredients. Cool completely.

Combine all ingredients except vanilla in top of double boiler. Beat at low speed for 30 seconds. Place over boiling water. Beat constantly at high speed for 7 minutes or until stiff. Remove from heat. Add vanilla and beat additional minute or until thick enough to spread

Mardi Gras King Cake

1		pkg dry yeast	4		eggs
¼	cup	warm water	2	tsp	butter, melted
6	tsp	milk, boiled then cooled			light corn syrup, for topping
4 to 5	cups	flour			colored sugar crystals (green, yellow, purple), for topping
½	lb	butter			
¾	cup	sugar			
¼	tsp	salt			

Preheat oven to 325°. Dissolve yeast in warm water. Add milk and about ½ cup of flour. In a large bowl, blend butter, sugar, salt, and eggs. Add yeast mixture and mix thoroughly. Gradually add 2½ cups of flour to make a stiff dough. Place in a large greased bowl and brush with melted butter. Cover with a damp cloth and allow to rise until double in size, about 3 hours. When risen, punch down. Use 1 cup or more of flour to knead dough and roll into a 4-foot long rope. Form into an oval on a 14- × 17-inch greased cookie sheet, connecting ends of the rope with a few drops of water.

Cover with a damp cloth and let rise until double in size, about 1 hour. Bake for 35 to 45 minutes or until lightly browned. Brush top of cake with corn syrup and sprinkle with colored sugar

Oatmeal Brownies

1	stick	butter melted	½	cup	cocoa
1	cup	sugar	½	tsp	baking powder
2		eggs well beaten	½	tsp	salt
1	tsp	vanilla	1	cup	quick oats, uncooked
½	cup	flour	½	cup	nuts, chopped

Combine ingredients in order listed. Mix well. Pour batter into a well greased baking dish. Bake at 375° for 45 minutes or done

Orange Glaze

1	cup	sugar		juice from 3 oranges
2	tbl	orange rind, grated		

Bring to a boil and pour over cake.

Pineapple-Coconut Icing

1	cup	crushed pineapple, drained	1	stick	butter
1	cup	coconut	1	tbl	flour

| 1 | cup | pecans, chopped | 2 | | eggs |
| 1½ | cups | sugar | | | |

Mix pineapple, coconut and pecans and set aside. Mix sugar, butter, flour and eggs. Cook until thick. Add pineaple mixture to cooked mixture and stir well.

Red Velvet Cake

2½	cups	cake flour (not self-rising) sifted	1½	cups	sugar
1	tsp	baking powder	2		eggs at room temperature
1	tsp	salt	1	tsp	vanilla
2	tbl	cocoa	1	cup	buttermilk at room temperature
1	2 oz bottle	red food coloring	1	tsp	white vinegar
1	stick	butter, unsalted room temperature	1	tsp	baking soda

Preheat oven to 350°. Butter and flour two 9-inch round cake pans or three 8-inch round cake pans. Sift together the cake flour, baking powder, and salt into a medium bowl; set aside. In a small bowl, mix food coloring and cocoa powder to form a thin paste without lumps; set aside. In a large bowl, using a hand mixer or stand mixer, beat butter and sugar together until light and fluffy, about three minutes. Beat in eggs, one at a time, then beat in vanilla and the red cocoa paste, scraping down the bowl with a spatula as you go. Add one third of the flour mixture to the butter mixture, beat well, then beat in half of the buttermilk. Beat in another third of flour mixture, then second half of buttermilk. End with the last third of the flour mixture, beat until well combined, making sure to scrape down the bowl with a spatula. Make sure you have cake pans buttered, floured, and nearby. In a small bowl, mix vinegar and baking soda. Yes, it will fizz! Add it to the cake batter and stir well to combine. Working quickly, divide batter evenly between the cake pans and place them in a preheated 350° oven. Bake for 25-30 minutes. Check early, cake is done when a toothpick inserted in the center comes out clean. Cool the cakes in their pans on a wire rack for 10 minutes. To remove the cakes from the pan, place a wire rack on top of the cake pan and invert, then gently lift the pan. Allow cakes to cool completely before frosting. Frost with butter cream or cream cheese icing

Robert E. Lee Cake

9		eggs separated	3		lemon zest
1½	cups	sugar	5		orange zest
2	cups	all purpose-flour sifted	½	cup	lemon juice divided
½	tsp	salt	2	cups	orange juice
Glaze			1½	cups	sugar
1	tbl	lemon juice	1½	cups	coconut shredded and divided

Preheat oven 350°. Grease and flour 3 8-inch round cake pans. In a 4-quart mixing bowl, beat egg whites until they just form stiff peaks. In a separate large bowl, beat egg yolks until light-colored. Slowly beat in sugar. Sift together flour, salt in a 1-quart mixing bowl and set aside. Using a rubber spatula, fold in egg whites, then flour mixture and1 tablespoon of the lemon juice, mixing only enough to blend in flour. Divide batter equally among the 3 cake pans. Bake until cake tester inserted in the middle comes out clean, about 35-45 minutes. Set pans on a wire rack to cool; after 10 minutes, remove cake layers from pans and place on wire rack to cool completely. In a 2-quart mixing bowl, combine citrus zest and juices, 1 sugar, and 1 cup of the coconut, stiring to dissolve sugar. Spoon citrus mixture over tops of cake layers. Stack layers and allow to stand several hours before serving to allow cake to absorb liquid. To serve, sprinkle with remaining 1/2 cup coconut.

Sour Cream Cake

3	cups	all purpose-flour sifted	2	sticks	butter (no substitutes), softened
¼	tsp	baking soda	6		eggs separated
3	cups	sugar	½	pint	sour cream

Cream butter and sugar. Add egg yolks one at a time. Add baking soda to sifted flour. Add flour and sour cream alternately. Beat egg whites (not to stiff) and fold into batter. Pour into a well greased and floured tube pan. Do Not Add Vanilla! Bake at 300° for 1½ to 1 ¾ hours. Remove immediately from pan to cool

Sour Cream Pound Cake

Louise Crews Aldridge

1	16 oz ctn	heavy whipping cream	3	cups	cake flour (not self-rising)
3	cups	sugar	1	8-oz ctn	sour cream
6		eggs	1	tsp	vanilla

Beat whipping cream until it turns to butter (takes maybe 15 minutes). Pour off the liquid. Add sugar and mix good, add eggs one at a time. Alternate cake flour with 8 oz sour cream ending with flour. Add vanilla. I sometimes will add chopped pecans. If you add pecans coat with a little of the flour. Bake in a greased and floured tube pan at 325 until golden brown and when a pick is inserted it comes out clean.

Sprite Cake

1	box	lemon supreme cake mix	4		eggs
1	box	lemon instant pudding	1	can	Sprite (may substitute 7-Up)
¾	cup	oil			

Mix all ingredients and beat for 3 minutes on medium speed. Pour into greased and floured cake pans. Bake at 350° for 25 to 30 minutes or until done. Frost with pineapple-coconut icing

Sugar-Free Fruitcake

2½	cups	candied fruits	3	packets	Equal
1	cup	raisins	3		eggs
½	cup	golden raisins	1½	tsp	cinnamon

½	cup	dried apricots	½	tsp	allspice
¼	cup	dark rum or orange juice	¼	tsp	ginger
½	cup	almonds chopped	1	stick	butter
1¼	cups	self rising flour	1	tsp	vanilla

In large bowl, combine candied fruits, dark and golden raisins, apricots and rum; set aside 30 minutes, stirring occasionally. Stir in almonds. Preheat oven to 300°. In medium bowl, combine flour, cinnamon, baking powder, allspice, ginger and salt; set aside. In large bowl, with electric mixer, beat margarine, sugar and Equal until light and fluffy. Add eggs, one at a time, beating well after each addition. Beat in vanilla. Beat in flour mixture, a small amount at a time until well blended. Stir in fruit mixture. Divide batter evenly between two loaf pans sprayed with non-stick vegetable cooking spray. Bake 1 hour 45 minutes, or until knife inserted in center comes out clean. Cool in pans 10 minutes. Remove from pans and cool on wire racks.

Tangle Cakes and Plow Rows

1	pint	sour milk	1	tsp	salt
3		eggs well beaten	1	lb	flour
½	tsp	baking soda			

Heat enough oil to cover the batter. Pour batter into hot oil and cook to a golden brown.(When poured into the oil in straight rows, the cakes are sometimes referred to as "plow rows". When poured in a zig-zag manner, they are called "tangle cakes")

Yummy Chocolate Cake

1	box	chocolate cake mix	1	cup	water
1	box	instant chocolate pudding	3		eggs
1	cup	mayonnaise			

Grease and flour 2 cake pans. Mix all ingredients on low speed just until blended. Beat at medium speed for 2 minutes. Pour into cake pans. Bake at 350° until cake springs back or knife inserted in middle comes out clean. Cool in pans for 10 minutes. remove then frost with desired frosting

Cookies and Candies

Chocolate Creams

1	cup	water	1	tsp	vanilla
1	cup	sugar	1	block	chocolate squares, melted
1	tbl	cornstarch			

Combine water, sugar and cornstarch and boil for 8 minutes. Remove from heat and beat until creamy. Add vanilla. Shape into balls and flatten with fork. Dip in chocolate and place on wax paper. Cool

Divinity

You CAN make this in the rain

2	cups	sugar	2		egg whites
1/3	cup	Karo syrup	½	cup	nuts, finely chopped (optional)
½	cup	boiling water			

Mix sugar, water and syrup and boil rapidly to hard ball stage. Pour slowly into well beaten egg whites. Beat until it begins to loose its gloss. Add nuts if desired and mix well. Spoon onto wax paper

Fruitcake Cookies

1	lb	butter	1	tsp	baking soda
1	lb	brown sugar	1	lb	raisins
3		eggs	1	lb	nuts (pecans or walnuts), chopped
1	tbl	milk	1	lb	candied cherries
5	cups	flour	1	lb	candied pineapple, diced
1		can shredded coconut			

Preheat oven to 375°. Measure 4 cups flour and mix with baking soda. Combine fruit, coconut, and nuts and mix with remaining 1 cup flour in a separate mixing bowl. Cream the butter, sugar, and milk together. Add the eggs one at a time. Beat in flour and baking soda mixture gradually, switching to a wooden spoon or spatula if batter becomes too stiff for the electric mixer. Stir fruit, coconut, and nut mixture into batter. Drop by teaspoonful onto greased cookie sheet. Bake for 10 minutes.

Ice Box Tea Cakes

2	cups	sugar, white, brown or mixed	3½	cups	self rising flour
2	sticks	butter	1	tsp	vanilla

2   eggs

Cream butter and sugar. Add eggs and remaining ingredients. Shape into log. Wrap in wax paper or cellophane wrap. Chill. Slice and bake at 350° until brown.

Dough will keep several days in refrigerator

Impossible Cookies

1	cup	peanut butter		1	cup	sugar
1		egg		½	tsp	vanilla

Beat together and form 1 inch balls. Place on greased cookie sheet allowing room to spread. Bake at 350° for 15 to 18 minutes

Just Cookies

2	sticks	butter		2	tsp	vanilla
1½	cups	sugar		2	cups	pecans, chopped
2		eggs		1	6 oz pkg	chocolate chips
3	cups	self rising flour				

Cream butter and sugar. Add eggs, flour and vanilla. Mix thoroughly. Add nuts and chocolate chips and stir with spoon to mix. Roll into balls and place on lightly greased cookie sheet. Flatten with finger tips. Bake at 325° until golden brown.

Marshmallow Fudge

2	cups	sugar		2	squares	chocolate
1	cup	milk		2	tbl	marshmallow creme
2	tbl	butter				

Combine, sugar, milk, butter and chocolate. Boil to soft ball stage. Remove from heat and beat rapidly until fudge begins to thicken. Add marshmallow creme and beat rapidly. Pour into greased dish and spread evenly. Work quickly before it hardens. Ground walnuts can be added if desired

Martha Washington Balls

1	box	powdered sugar		½	block	Bakers unsweetened chocolate
1½	cups	nuts, chopped		½	stick	parafin wax
½	can	Eagle Brand Milk		1	tsp	flavoring of choice

Mix sugar, nuts, Eagle Brand milk and flavoring and roll into balls. Melt chocolate and wax in double boiler (can place boiler over a pot with boiling water). Dip balls in chocolate mixture. Let cool

Mock Peanut Brittle

½	cup	sugar	½ cup	crunchy peanut butter
½	cup	Karo Syrup	5 cups	corn flakes

Boil sugar and syrup until sugar dissolves. Remove from heat and stir in peanut butter. Stir in corn flakes. Press into greased pan. Cut into squares while warm

Nut Candy

2	cups	sugar	½	cup	milk
2	tbl	molasses	2	squares	chocolate
2	tbl	butter	½	cup	walnuts, roughly chopped

Mix all ingredients except nuts. Boil over medium heat to soft ball stage. Stir constantly to avoid scorching. Add nuts and stir. Drop by spoonfuls onto wax paper. Cool

Nut Macaroons

1	lb	nuts, finely chopped	1	box	10 X sugar
5		egg whites			

Mix all ingredients and beat until stiff. Drop by spoonfuls onto lightly greased cookie sheet. Bake at 350° until brown

Peanut Brittle

O.H. and Sarah King

2	cups	peanuts	½	cup	water
½	cup	white Karo syrup	1	heaping tbl	butter
¼	tsp	salt	1 or 2		buttered cookie sheets
2	tbl	baking soda			heavy saucepan
1½	cups	sugar			

Put peanuts, sugar and water in heavy saucepan. Begin cooking at medium high temperature until ingredients begin to bubble good (approximately 200°). Turn down to medium heat until peanuts begin to brown lightly. Turn up to medium high heat until finished cooking. (with some peanuts you may have to turn temperature up the second time).

Move spoon around in peanuts and syrup only enough to uniformly cook peanuts. When temperature reaches approximately 250-260° add salt and butter. Mix uniformly. When temperature reaches 290° (hard crack) add soda. Mix thoroughly. Remove from heat and immediately pour on buttered cookie sheet as thinly as possible. As the candy begins to cool, stretch working from the edges toward the middle. When cool, break and put in container which can be closed.

Peanut Butter Balls

1 cup peanut butter
½ cup honey
1 cup quick oats, uncooked
1 cup mixed dried fruit, chopped
½ cup wheat germ
coconut
red and green food coloring
peanuts, chopped

Combine peanut butter, honey, oats, dried fruit and wheat germ. Mix well with spoon. Shape into balls. Roll in mixture of coconut, food colorings and chopped nuts.

Peanut Butter Chocolate Fudge

2 cups sugar
¾ cup milk
2 tbl corn syrup
¼ cup peanut butter
1 tsp vanilla
dash salt
4 tbl cocoa

Boil sugar, milk, corn syrup and cocoa to soft stage. Let stand without beating until cool. Add peanut butter, vanilla and salt but do not stir. Beat until creamy. Pour into a buttered pan until cool. Cut in squares

Peanut Fudge

2 cups sugar
½ cup milk
2 tbl peanut butter

Boil to a soft ball stage. Beat mixture and pour into buttered casserole dish. Cut into squares

Popcorn Balls

popcorn
½ cup sugar
½ cup molasses
¾ stick butter

Pop desired amount of popcorn. Mix all other ingredients and boil to hard ball stage. Stir into popcorn and shape into balls

Rolled Oats Candy

1 cup oats
1 egg yolk
1 tbl water
1 tbl brown sugar
½ cup karo syrup
1 egg white, stiffly beaten

Brown oats on pie plate in oven. Beat egg yolk. Add water and stir. Combine with oats. Beat egg white and add brown sugar, karo syrup and mix with oats. Roll into balls. If mixture is not thick enough add more oats. Place balls on butter cookie sheet. Bake at 350° until crisp

Sand Tarts

1	cup	butter		2	tsp	vanilla
5	tbl	powdered sugar		1½	cups	nuts, chopped
2	cups	self rising flour				

Cream butter and sugar then add vanilla and flour. Mix. Add nuts into creamed mixture.. Form into small balls. Bake at 325° for 30 minutes. When done, roll in powdered sugar while hot

Seafoam

2	cups	sugar		1	tsp	vanilla
2	tbl	molasses		½	cup	nuts, chopped
1		egg white				

Mix, sugar, molasses and egg white. Cook over medium heat to soft ball stage. Add vanilla. Mix in the nuts. Drop by spoonfuls on wax paper. Let cool

Special K Candy

1	cup	karo syrup		1	16 oz jar	peanut butter
1	cup	sugar		2½	cups	Special K cereal

Bring syrup and sugar to a boil. Add peanut butter and stir until it melts. Add cereal and mix well. Drop by spoonfuls onto wax paper. Let cook

Tea Cakes

1	cup	butter		1 tbl	vanilla
2	cups	sugar			flour to mix
3		eggs			

Mix butter, sugar, vanilla and eggs thoroughly. Add flour until it makes a soft dough. Roll out small amounts of dough in palm of hand then flatten. Place on lightly greased cookie sheet and bake at 325° until golden brown

Pies

Buttermilk Pie

¼	cup	flour		½	tsp	vanilla
½	cup	butter (no substitutes), melted		3	lg	eggs
½	cup	buttermilk		1		deep dish unbaked pie shell
1½	cups	sugar				

Mix all ingredients with whisk and pour into pie shell. Bake in deep dish pie shell at 350° for 50 to 60 minutes. Pie is done when golden brown and toothpick comes out clean when inserted in middle of pie

Cherry Cheese Pie

1 9 inch	graham cracker crust		1/3	cup	Real Lemon juice from concentrate
1 8 oz pkg	cream cheese, softened		1	tsp	vanilla
1 can	Eagle Brand Milk		1	21 oz can	cherry pie filling chilled

In a large mixer bowl, beat cheese until fluffy. Gradually beat in Eagle Brand until smooth. Stir in Real Lemon and vanilla. Pour into prepared crust and chill about three hours. Top with pie filling before serving.

Chocolate Chess Pie

1	tbl	sugar		½	cup	pecans, chopped
4	tbl	cocoa		3		eggs beaten
	pinch	salt		½	cup	milk
1	tbl	all purpose flour		1	tbl	vanilla
1	tbl	cornmeal		1	9 inch	pie shell, unbaked

Combine first 6 ingredients in medium bowl and mix well. Combine eggs, milk and vanilla into and add to dry ingredients and mix well. Pour into pie shell and bake for 45 to 50 minutes at 350° or until pie is set.

Mock Apple Pie

2		pastry crusts		2	tbl	lemon juice
36		Ritz Crackers coarsely broken		1		lemon peel, freshly grated
1¾	cups	cold water		2	tbl	butter
2	cups	sugar		½	tsp	cinnamon
2	tsp	cream of tarter				

Roll out half the pastry and line a 9-inch pie plate. Place cracker crumbs in prepared crust; set aside. Heat water, sugar and cream of tartar to a boil in saucepan over high heat; simmer for 15 minutes. Add lemon juice and peel; cool. Pour syrup over cracker crumbs. Dot with margarine or butter; sprinkle with cinnamon. Roll out remaining pastry; place over pie. Trim, seal and flute edges. Slit top crust to allow steam to escape. Bake at 425° for 30 to 35 minutes or until crust is crisp and golden. Cool completely.

Old Fashion Egg Pie

1	cup	sugar	2	tbl	butter (no substitutes), melted
2½	tbl	flour	1		deep dish unbaked pie shell
1¼	tsp	nutmeg			
4		egg yolks			
2		egg whites			
1	cup	milk			

Meringue

2		egg whites
2	tbl	sugar

Mix all ingredients thoroughly and pour into unbaked pie shell. Bake at 350° for approximately 1 hour or until knife come out clean when inserted in middle of pie. Make meringue of 2 egg whites and 2 tbl sugar. Beat until stiff peak forms.

Ole Time Lemon Pie

1 1/3	cups	sugar	1½	tsp	lemon peel, freshly grated
1¼	cup	water	1		pie shell baked
2	tbl	butter			
1/3	cup	cornstarch			
½	cup	ice water			
4		egg yolks lightly beaten			
3	tbl	milk			
¼	cup	lemon juice, freshly squeezed			

Meringue

4		egg whites
½	cup	sugar
1	tsp	lemon juice, freshly squeezed

Combine sugar, water and butter. Heat until sugar dissolves. Blend cornstarch in ice water and add to mixture. Cook slowly, stirring constantly until clear (about 8 minutes). Slowly stir in egg yolks which have been beaten with milk. Cook 2 minutes, stirring constantly. Remove from heat. Add lemon juice and peel. Cool. Pour into cooled pie shell. Beat egg whites until stiff. Gradually add sugar then lemon juice. Spread over cooled filling and brown at 350° for about 15 minutes

Ozark Pie

Louise Crews Aldridge

1	cup	sugar	1		apple chopped (I like mine chopped fine) red or golden delicious
1	cup	self rising flour	1	cup	pecans, chopped
1	stick	butter, melted			
1		egg			

1   tsp   vanilla

Mix all of the above. Spray a 9 inch pie pan and bake until golden brown at 325°. I use the disposable pie pans a lot for these as I give them as gifts.

Peanut Butter Ice Box Pie

1	sm block	cream cheese		1	8 oz ctn	frozen whipped topping
1/3	cup	crunchy peanut butter		1	9 inch	graham cracker crust
1	cup	powdered sugar				

Blend cream cheese with peanut butter. Add sugar and mix well. Fold in whipped topping. Pour into pie crust. Garnish with chopped peanuts if desired Cool in refrigerator

Pecan And Walnut Pie

1 1/4	cups	light corn syrup		1/4	tsp	kosher salt
1/2	cup	packed dark brown sugar		1	cup	pecan halves
1/4	cup	granulated sugar		1	cup	walnut halves
3		large eggs		1		piecrust (store-bought refrigerated rolled or homemade), fitted into a 9-inch pie plate
2	tbl	unsalted butter, melted				
2	tsp	pure vanilla extract				

Heat oven to 350°. In a large bowl, whisk together the corn syrup, brown and granulated sugars, eggs, butter, vanilla, and salt. Mix in the pecans and walnuts. Place the pie plate on a rimmed baking sheet. Fill with the nut mixture and bake until the center is set, 45 to 50 minutes. Let cool completely before serving.

Pecan Pie

1	cup	brown sugar		2	tbl	butter
3		eggs		1	tsp	vanilla
1	tbl	self rising flour		1½	cups	pecans
1	cup	dark corn syrup		1		pie shell, deepdish, unbaked

Preheat oven to 350°. Place pie shell in a 9 inch pie pan. In a medium bowl, gently beat eggs. Stir in sugar and flour, then the syrup, butter and vanilla. Fold in pecans. Pour mixture into pie shell. Bake for 60 to 70 minutes; knife inserted in center of pie should come out clean.

Spiced Pumpkin Cheesecake

38		ginger snaps, finely crushed (about 1-1/2 cups)		1	15-oz can	pumpkin
				1	tbl	pumpkin pie spice
1/4	cup	finely chopped pecans		1	tsp	vanilla
1/4	cup	butter or margarine, melted		4		eggs
4	8 oz pkg	cream cheese, softened		1/2	tsp	nutmeg

1	cup	sugar

Heat oven to 325°. Mix crumbs, nuts and butter; press onto bottom and 1 inch up side of 9-inch springform pan.

Beat cream cheese and sugar in large bowl with mixer until well blended. Add pumpkin, spice and vanilla; mix well. Add eggs, 1 at a time, mixing on low speed after each just until blended. Pour into crust.

Bake 1 hour 20 min. to 1 hour 30 min. or until center is almost set. Loosen cake from rim of pan; cool before removing rim. Refrigerate 4 hours.

Strawberry Dessert

1	cup	sugar	3	tbl	cornstarch
1	cup	water	4	tbl	strawberry jello

Mix cornstarch with sugar and water and cook until thickened. Remove from stove and add jello. Cool and pour over strawberries. Placed in a cooked pie shell. Cool in refrigerator

Sweet Potato Pie

2	cups	sweet potatoes, boiled, peeled and mashed	¼	tsp	salt
¾	cup	brown sugar firmly packed	½	stick	butter (no substitutes), melted
½	cup	sugar	2	5 oz cans	evaporated milk
1¼	tsp	allspice	3	lg	eggs
½	tsp	nutmeg	1	tbl	vanilla
1	tsp	cinnamon			

Boil two medium sweet potatoes in their jackets in a covered pot over moderate flame, until sweet potatoes are very soft and tender. Remove potatoes from the water and allow to cool on a plate or wire rack. When cool enough to handle, peel potatoes, cut into chunks and place in a large bowl. Mash potatoes thoroughly with a potato masher. There should be NO lumps. Measure 2 cups of the potatoes and put in a medium sized pot with the packed brown sugar, all of the spices, salt, the 1/2 stick butter, and one 5 oz can of evaporated milk. Cook on low flame for about 5 minutes, whipping with a wire whisk until butter and brown sugar are melted down and mixture is well blended, smooth and starts to bubble. Remove from fire and let cool in pot. In a medium sized bowl, beat the three eggs with a fork. Add the second 5oz can of evaporated milk, granulated sugar and vanilla to the eggs and continue beating until creamy. Pour the cooled sweet potato mixture from pot into a large bowl. Stir in the egg mixture. Blend thoroughly with a whisk. Pour into deepdish pie shell and bake at 375° until set

Traditional Pumpkin Pie

1	9 inch	unbaked pie shell	1	tsp	cinnamon
1	16 oz can	pumpkin	½	tsp	ginger
1	can	Eagle Brand Milk	½	tsp	nutmeg

2		eggs	½	tsp	salt

Preheat oven to 425°. In a large mixer bowl, combine all ingredient and mix well. Pour onto pastry shell. Bake 15 minutes and reduce oven temperature to 350° and bake for 35 to 40 minutes longer or until knife inserted 1 inch from edge comes out clean. Garnish as desired. Refrigerate leftovers.

Vinegar Pie

Don't judge a recipe by its name!

1	9 inch	pie shell, unbaked	½	cup	cider vinegar
1¼	cups	sugar	2	cups	water
¼	cup	flour	3	lg	eggs, well beaten
1	tbl	grated lemon zest	1	tbl	butter

Preheat the oven to 425°. Combine sugar, flour, and lemon zest in a saucepan and stir until thoroughly blended. Add cider vinegar while stirring or whisking constantly. Add the water. Place over medium heat, bring to a boil and cook, stirring constantly for 1 minute. Remove from heat and stir a little of the hot mixture into the eggs. Stir the warmed egg mixture into remaining hot mixture. Stir in butter. Pour the mixture into the prepared pie shell & bake for 10 minutes at 425° then reduce heat to 350°. Continue baking for 30 minutes more. Remove pie from oven and let it cool completely before serving. The filling will seem quite liquid, but will firm as the pie cools. Do Not Pre Bake the Pie Crust!!!!!

Puddings and Cobblers

Banana Pudding

3/4	cup	sugar	4		eggs
3	tbl	flour	1	tsp	vanilla
1/4	tsp	salt			vanilla wafers
2	cups	milk (add more if needed)			bananas

Before I begin I layer my bananas and wafers in a dish.

In a heavy boiler combine sugar, flour and salt and eggs. Whisk together then add milk. Cook over medium heat whisking CONSTANTLY until thick. Watch it closely as it will scorch. I use a WHISK. When pudding reaches desired thickness immediately pour over layered bananas and wafers. Ready to eat hot or cold!

You can make a meringue out of egg whites and sugar but I prefer it without

Bread Pudding

		bread cubes	1	cup	sugar
3	pints	milk	½		raisins

Fill buttered baking dish half full with bread cubes. Add milk, raisins and sugar Bake for 30 minutes at 350°. Serve with whipped cream on top

Caramel Pudding

2	cups	brown sugar	2		egg yolks well beaten
¾	stick	butter	4	tbl	milk
3	pints	milk	1	tsp	vanilla
4	tbl	flour			

Brown sugar and butter over low heat. Add 3 pints milk. Add egg yolks, 4 tbs milk, vanilla and flour. Mix well and pour into greased baking dish. Bake at 400° until brown

Chocolate Pudding

4	tbl	cocoa	2		eggs
3	tbl	flour	2	cups	milk
1	cup	sugar	1	tsp	vanilla

Mix cocoa, flour and sugar until lumps are gone. I usually whisk it. Add eggs and milk. Mix well. Cook in heavy boiler on medium heat. Whisk constantly until thick. Remove from heat and add vanilla. Stir to blend. Let cool

Cottage Pudding

1	cup	flour	½	cup	milk
½	cup	sugar	1		egg
	pinch	salt	2	tbl	butter melted
2	tbl	baking powder			

Mix all ingredients together. Pour into greased baking dish and bake at 325° until brown. Serve with additional milk and sugar

Cracker Pudding

1	quart	milk	¾	cup	coconut shredded
2		egg yolks well beaten	1½	cups	cracker crumbs
¾	cup	sugar	1	tsp	vanilla

Beat egg yolks and sugar together; pour into double boiler and add milk. Stir constantly so it doesn't burn. Add crackers and coconut cook until thickened. Remove from heat and add vanilla (and salt, if needed). Cool and then chill in refrigerator.

Crow's Nest Pudding

1	pinch	cherries, pitted, coarsely chopped, and drained	1	cup	sugar
2	tsp	flour	1		golf ball size butter
3	tbl	sugar	1	tsp	baking powder
Batter			½	cup	milk
1		egg	1	tsp	vanilla

Put cherries in bottom of greased baking dish. Sprinkle flour and sugar on top. Make a batter of egg, sugar, baking powder, butter, milk and vanilla. Pour over cherries and bake at 350° for 30 to 40 minutes or until brown and bubbly.

Can substitute apple, peach or blueberry pie filling

Easy Peach Dessert

1	lg can	sliced peaches, undrained	1	cup	pecans, chopped
1	box	yellow cake mix	1	stick	butter (or margarine) melted
1	cup	coconut			

Spread peaches in bottom of 13 X 9 inch pan. Sprinkle dry cake mix over peaches. Combine coconut and pecans and sprinkle over cake mix. Dot top with melted margarine. Bake at 350° for 50-50 minutes.

Family Size Banana Pudding

1½	cups	sugar	2	tsp	vanilla
6	tbs	flour	8		eggs
½	tsp	salt	8 to 10		bananas, sliced
4	cups	milk	1	lg bag	vanilla wafers

Mix all ingredients except vanilla, bananas and wafers in heavy boiler. Stir constantly (I use a whisk) over medium heat until thick. Add vanilla. Pour over layers of bananas and wafers.

Mom's Apple Cobbler

1	stick	butter	½	cup	shortening
2	cups	sugar	½	cup	milk
2	cups	water	2	cups	apples, peeled, cored and finely chopped
1½	cups	self-rising flour	1	tsp	cinnamon

Preheat oven to 350°. Melt butter in a baking dish or sheet cake pan. In a sauce pan, heat sugar and water until sugar melts. Cut shortening into flour until particles are like crumbs. Add milk and stir with a fork only until dough leaves the side of the bowl. Turn out onto lightly floured board or pastry cloth and kneed until smooth. Roll dough out into a large rectangle. Sprinkle cinnamon over apple the sprinkle apples over dough. Roll up like a jelly roll, dampen the edge with a little water and seal. Slice dough into about 16 slices. Place in pan with melted butter and pour sugar syrup carefully around rolls. Bake for 55-60 minutes

Peach Cobbler

1	cup	flour	1	stick	butter
1	cup	sugar	1	tsp	vanilla
1	cup	milk	1	lg can	peach slices with juice

Melt butter in a large baking dish. Mix flour, sugar, milk and vanilla in a bowl. Pour over melted butter. Pour peaches and juice over batter. Bake at 425° until top is golden brown and bubbly. Crust will rise to the top during baking. I always put foil on rack under the dish to catch any overspill

Rice Pudding

1/3	cup	rice	½	tsp	salt
4	cups	milk	1/3	cup	sugar

Place rice in milk. Add salt and sugar. Mix and pour in buttered dish. Bake for 3 hours at 300°

Jams, Jellies, Pickles and Preserves

Apple Butter

7	cups	apple pulp		4	lbs	sugar
1	tsp	cinnamon		1	pkg	sure-gel
½	tsp	cloves				

Mix sure gel with pulp in large boiler. Bring to a boil stirring frequently to avoid scorching. Add sugar and bring to rolling boil. Boil for 1 to 2 minutes or until sugar is fully dissolved. Pour into jars and seal

Apple Jelly

apple juice		1 pkg	sure-gel
sugar			

Mix equal parts apple juice and sugar. Bring to a boil and add pectin. Boil until thick. Pour into sterile jars and seal

Apricot Jam

2	lbs	apricots, peeled		3	tbl	lemon juice
1½	cups	sugar		1	pkg	pectin or sure gel

Skin 2 pounds of fresh apricots. Cut in half and remove pits. Add sugar and lemon juice. Cook over low heat and when mixture comes to a boil, stir. Add pectin. Stir constantly until it thickens. Store in sterile, sealed jars

Cinnamon Pickles

2	gallons	cucumbers peeled and cut into 1/4-inch slices		2	cups	water
				1½	oz	red food coloring
8	quarts	water		10	cups	sugar
2	cups	pickling lime		6	sticks	cinnamon
1	tbl	alum		10	oz	red hot candies
2	cups	vinegar				

Prepare the cucumbers: peel, removed ends, core, and cut into rings or sticks. Combine water and lime. Soak prepared cucumbers in lime water for 24 hours. Drain and wash 3 times in cold water. Cover with cold water and let sit for 3 hours. Combine alum, vinegar, 2 cups water, food coloring, sugar, cinnamon and red hots to make a syrup. Add drained cucumbers and simmer, covered, for 2 hours. Let stand overnight. Drain off syrup, reheat and pour over pickles daily for 3 days. Pack in hot jars and seal.

Cinnamon Red Hots

1	gallon	cucumbers peeled and sliced
2	cups	pickling lime
2	cups	vinegar
2	cups	water

1	bag	cinnamon red hot candies
8	cups	sugar
8	sticks	cinnamon
1	bottle	red food coloring

Day 1 Soak cucumber slices for 24 hours in water to cover with 2 cups pickling lime. Day 2 drain and rinse thoroughly. Soak in clear water for 3 hours and drain. Mix vinegar, 2 cups water, red hot candy, sugar, cinnamon and red food coloring and bring to a boil. Pour over cucumber.

Day 3 Reheat cucumbers to boiling then cool (do not drain) Day 4 Reheat cucumbers to boiling and place in jars. Tighten lids and process in hot water bath

Easy Sweet Pickles

1 jar dill pickles, drained	sugar to cover

Pour liquid from dill pickles. Pour sugar over pickles until covered. Put lid back on jar. Let sugar dissolve over pickles (will take several days). Pickles will be sweet when opened. Do Not Refrigerate while sugar is dissolving

Green Tomato Marmalade

2	lbs	green tomatoes chopped
1	lb	sugar
¼	tsp	salt

1	pkg	pectin or sure-gel
3		lemons peeled and thinly sliced

Cut green tomatoes into small pieces. Add sugar and salt. Remove the peel from three lemons and cut into thin slices. Boil peel in water until tender. Slice lemon into thin slices, removing the seed. Bring lemon slices to a boil and combine the tomato mixture with lemon slices and peel. Add pectin. Boil for one hour or until the mixture thickens. Pour at once into sterile jars and seal.

Green Tomato Pickle

8	quarts	green tomatoes			cloves
		salt			allspice
		vinegar			whole ginger
6		onions diced	1	oz	mustard seed
6		bell peppers diced	1 1/2	lbs	brown sugar

tumeric	Coleman's mustard
celery seed	flour

Wash and cut 8 quarts of tomatoes into quarters. Sprinkle them with salt and let stand for 12 hours. Drain and cover with vinegar.

Add onions and peppers and 1 tsp of the following spices tumeric, celery seed, cloves, allspice and whole ginger. Mustard seed and brown sugar should be included when the mixture comes to a boil. After cooking (low heat) for 2 hours, add Coleman's mustard and thicken mixture with a small amount of flour.

Seal in jars.

Pepper Jelly

¾	cup	bell pepper, chopped	5	cups	sugar
¼	cup	hot pepper	1	pkg	sure-gel
1½	cups	vinegar	1	cup	water

Chop all pepper before measuring. Boil all ingredients 2 minutes. Remove from heat. Dissolve sure jell in 1 cup water. Gradually add to pepper mixture. Stir constantly for 5 minutes. Pour into jars.

Pepper Relish

24		bell pepper, seeded and chopped	1	pinch	vinegar
12		onion peeled and chopped	2	tsp	salt
2½	lbs	sugar			

Grind peppers and onions. Cover with cold water for 20 minutes. Drain and squeeze out water. Mix sugar, vinegar and salt then add pepper and onions. Bring to a boil and simmer for 30 minutes. Put in jars and seal

Pickled Beets

3	quarts	cooked beets-peeled and cut up	1½	cups	water or beet brine
4	cups	sugar	2	tbl	salt
3	cups	vinegar			

Heat sugar, vinegar, water (brine) and salt to boiling. Put cooked beets in jars. Pour boiling syrup over beets until covered. Leave ½" headroom in jars. Put lids on and process in boiling water bath for 30 minutes. Lids will seal with a pop.

Pickled Okra

3	quarts	young okra pods	6		garlic cloves, peeled
1	quart	white vinegar	6		hot peppers
1	cup	water	6	tsp	dill seed

½ cup   salt

Wash and sterilize 6 pint jars. Place a garlic clove and a hot pepper in each jar. Bring vinegar, water and salt to a boil. Simmer for 5 minutes. Pour liquid into jars packed with okra. Seal jars and put in a boiling water bath for 10 minutes. Lids will seal during boiling

Pickled Radishes and Green Beans

2	cups	white vinegar		1	tbl	kosher salt
1/2	cup	water		1	lb	radishes, trimmed
2	tbl	sugar		1/2	lb	green beans, trimmed
2	tsp	whole black peppercorns				zest of 1 lemon
5		garlic cloves, peeled and smashed				

In a saucepan, combine vinegar, water, sugar, whole black peppercorns, garlic cloves, and kosher salt and bring to a boil. Remove from heat and let sit for 15 minutes.

Meanwhile, combine the radishes, trimmed green beans, lemon zest in a large bowl. Add the vinegar mixture and let sit 15 minutes.

Plum Jam

2	lbs	large plums		5½	cups	sugar
2	cups	water		1	pkg	pectin or sure-gel

Combine and cook plums in two cups of water until fruit is soft. Add sugar and pectin. Boil for fifteen minutes, strain through a sieve, removing pits and skins. Continue cooking until mixture thickens. Pour into sterile, sealed jars

Relish

1	gallon	green tomatoes chopped		1	tbl	mustard
12		onions finely chopped		½	tsp	cloves
6		mild peppers		½	tsp	ginger
½	cup	salt				brown sugar
1	tbl	celery seed				vinegar

Mix green tomatoes, chopped onions, peppers, salt, celery seed, mustard, cloves and ginger. Bring to a boil. Add enough brown sugar to taste and enough vinegar to cover the contents. Continue cooking ½ hour. Place contents in pint jars and seal.

Spiced Peaches

3	lbs	sugar		6	lbs	peaches
1	cup	vinegar		2	doz	cloves
1	doz	sticks cinnamon				

Cook together sugar, vinegar and cinnamon. When boiling, add peeled peaches and cook until the fruit is soft. Remove the peaches, but continue cooking the liquid adding cloves. Pack the peaches in sterile jars, pour the liquid (syrup) over the peaches and seal.

Strawberry Fig Preserves

6	cups	figs, peeled
6	cups	sugar
1	cup	water

3	3-ounce boxes	strawberry Jello
1	box	sure-gel

Boil figs, sugar and water for 30 minutes. Add 3 boxes strawberry Jello and 1 box Sur-Jell. Cook until figs are tender. Stir constantly to avoid sticking. Put in jars and seal.

Strawberry Jelly

2	cups	fresh strawberries
1	cup	water

3	cups	sugar

Cut fresh strawberries. Boil for thirty minutes in one cup of water and three cups of sugar. Add pectin and cook until mixture thickens. Pour into sterile jars and seal (Strain if clear jelly is desired)

Sweet Orange Marmalade

6		oranges
3	lbs	sugar

		water
1	pkg	pectin or sure-gel

Peel two oranges and slice peel thin, in narrow strips. And cover with water, boil until tender. Peel four oranges, boil the pulp in two quarts water until soft. Strain through a sieve. Mix with the prepared peel, add three pounds of sugar and pectin. Cook until mixture thickens When mixture cools slightly, pour into sterile, sealed jars

Vidalia Onion Relish

6	lg	Vidalia onions, finely chopped
6		red bell peppers finely chopped
1	quart	vinegar

6		green bell peppers, chopped
2	tbl	salt
1	cup	sugar

Combine all ingredients, bring to a boil. Cook until slightly thickened, about 25 minutes, stirring occasionally. Pack hot in preheated jars, leaving 1/4 inch of head space. Fill and close jars. Process for 10 minutes. Cool and store. Makes about 5 pints.

Main Dishes

 Beef

Beef and Beans

1		onion chopped
1		bell pepper, chopped
2	tbl	butter
1	lb	ground beef
1	can	pork n beans

1	can	tomatoes, diced
1	cup	rice, cooked
1	tsp	salt
1	tsp	pepper
1	tsp	chili powder

Brown onion and bell pepper in butter. Add beef and cook until brown. Drain. Add beans, tomatoes, rice, salt, pepper and chili powder. Simmer for 30 minutes

Beef and Wild Rice Casserole

1	box	wild rice, soaked in water and drained
1	lb	ground beef
¼	cup	onion chopped
¼	cup	bell pepper, chopped

1	can	cream of mushroom soup
2	tbl	butter
2	tbl	soy sauce
2½	cups	water

Brown onion, bell pepper and beef in butter. Drain if needed. Add soup, soy sauce, water and rice. Bake uncovered at 350° for 1 ½ hours or until rice is tender

Beef Bean Dish

1		onion (chopped)
1		bell pepper (chopped)
1	tbl	butter
½	lb	beef
1		can kidney beans

1		can tomatoes
1	cup	cooked rice
1	tsp	salt
½	tsp	pepper
½	tsp	chili powder

Brown onion and bell pepper in butter. Add beef and cook until brown. Add beans, tomatoes, rice, salt, pepper and chili powder. Let simmer 30 minutes and serve with garlic bread.

Beef Casserole

2½	lbs	ground beef
1	tsp	garlic powder
2	sm can	tomato sauce
1	tsp	sugar
1	8-oz	cream cheese
1	16 oz ctn	sour cream

1	cup	cheddar cheese grated
4		bell pepper, chopped
1	10 oz pkg	egg noodles, uncooked
		Salt and black pepper to taste
1	can	cream of mushroom soup

Brown meat and drain. Add garlic, tomato sauce, salt, pepper and sugar. Simmer for 15 minutes. In bowl mix cream cheese, sour cream and onions. Cook noodles and drain. In large baking dish layer noodles, meat, grated cheese and sour cream mixture until all is used. Top with undiluted soup. Bake at 325° for 30 minutes or until bubbly. Sprinkle with additional cheese and let melt.

Beefy Hominy Casserole

1	lb	lean ground beef	1	can	cream of chicken soup
1/2	cup	onion chopped	1	can	yellow hominy drained
1	can	chili with beans	2	tbl	sliced ripe olives
2	tsp	chili powder	1/2	cup	shredded process cheese or Velveeta

Cook ground beef and onion till meat is browned. Stir in remaining ingredients, except the cheese. Spoon beef and hominy mixture into 2-quart casserole. Cover and bake at 350° for 25 minutes. Sprinkle cheese over top; continue baking, uncovered, for 5 to 10 minutes longer.

Bonanza Cheeseburgers

1	lb	ground chuck	**Filling**		
¼	tsp	salt	½	cup	grated cheddar cheese
½	cup	Quaker Oats	1	tbl	mayonnaise
¼	cup	chili sauce	½	tsp	Worcestershire sauce
2	tbl	milk	¼	tsp	prepared mustard
2	tsp	instant minced onion	½	tsp	season salt
2	tsp	Worcestershire sauce			

Combine meat, salt, oats, chili sauce, milk, onion and Worcestershire thoroughly. Shape to form 12 thin patties. Combine filling ingredients thoroughly. Spread about 1 ½ tsp on center of patties. Cover with remaining patties, pinch edges together to seal. Cook over hot coals or in broiler about 4 inches from source of meat. Cook about 5 minutes. Turn and cook 5 minutes longer. Serve on toasted buns.

Cheesy Meatloaf

1 1/2	lbs	lean ground beef	2	cups	Ritz crackers (crushed)
1		beaten egg	1/4	cup	onion
1/2	tsp	sage	1/2	cup	swiss cheese (shredded) plus some extra
1/2	cup	evaporated milk			salt and pepper

Mix all above together; pat into an oval loaf in a baking dish. Put the extra shredded Swiss cheese over top of loaf. Bake at 350° for 1 hour.

Chili

2	lbs	ground beef	3	tbs	chili powder
1	sm can	mushrooms	1	tsp	red pepper
1	med	onion chopped	3	cans	pork n beans
		Salt and black pepper to taste	1	sm can	tomato sauce
1	tsp	oregano	1	can	tomatoes, diced
1	tsp	garlic powder			

Brown meat with onions and drain. Add remaining ingredients. Add more spices to taste. Add small amounts of water if needed. Simmer 20 to 25 minutes.

Chuck Roast

2	lg slices	chuck roast 2 inches thick	2	tbl	vinegar
		meat tenderizer	2	tbl	Worcestershire sauce
¼	cup	soy sauce	2	tsp	garlic salt

Sprinkle meat tenderizer generously on both sides of chuck roast and spear with fork. Combine other ingredients and pour over roast. Marinate 12 hours in refrigerator.

Remove and leave at room temperature for 6 hours, turning meat in sauce every hour.

Place on charcoal grill 8 inches from coals. Broil ½ hour on each side for medium done steaks. Baste with left over sauce if more prominent flavors are desired.

Corned Beef Recipe for Crock Pots

4-1/2	lb	corned beef brisket	2	med	onions quartered
1	cup	water	2	lg	new potatoes cubed
3	tbl	apple cider vinegar	2		carrots (cubed)
3	tbl	sugar	1	head	cabbage, cut into small wedges
1/2	tsp	pepper			

In a lightly greased crock pot, add your corned beef brisket.

In a small bowl mix together, water, vinegar, sugar and pepper. Pour the mixture on top of the corn beef brisket. Cover the crock pot with a lid and cook on low heat for 10 to 12 hours. Add onions, potatoes, and carrots about 1-1/2 hours before the corned beef is done. Add cabbage 45 minutes before the corned beef is done.

Country Casserole

1	lb	beef chunks or ground beef	1	lb	egg noodles
1		chopped onion	1		can cream of mushroom soup
1		can tomato soup	1	tbl	olive oil

Saute' chopped onion in olive oil. Add beef. Cook well. Add can of tomato soup undiluted. Cook egg noodles according to directions on package. Drain well. Add can of cream of mushroom soup, undiluted. Grease casserole dish. Place 1/2 of beef mixture in bottom of casserole. Add 1/2 of noodle mixture. Put rest of beef on noodles. Add remaining noodles. If desired, sprinkle paprika lightly over top of noodles. Bake in 375° oven for 20-25 minutes, or until bubbly

Country Pie

1	lb	ground beef	1	tsp	pepper
½	cup	bread crumbs	1	lg can	tomato sauce
¼	cup	onion chopped	3	cups	rice, cooked
1	tsp	salt	½	cup	cheddar cheese grated

Mix beef, bread crumbs, onions, pepper and salt and ¼ cup tomato sauce. Spread in the bottom of a pie pan forming a shell. Mix rice, cheese and remaining tomato sauce. Place in meat shell. Sprinkle with grated cheese. Bake at 350° for 35 to 40 minutes or until meat is done. Drain excess grease while cooking. Cut into wedges and serve hot

Cumin Ground Beef Casserole

1	lb	ground beef	1¼	cups	rice, uncooked
½	cup	onion chopped	1	tsp	cumin
2	cans	beef broth			

Brown meat and onion then drain. Salt and pepper to taste. Add rest of ingredients and mix well. Put mixture into covered casserole dish and bake at 350° for 45 minutes or until rice is tender

Easy Hamburger Casserole

1	lb	ground beef	1	can	cream of mushroom soup
3	lg	potatos peeled and sliced	1	lg	onion chopped

Brown hamburger. Layer in casserole dish hamburger, onion and potatoes. Continue to layer until all ingredients have been used. Pour 1 can of mushroom soup over top. Bake at 350° degrees for approximately 1 hour until potatoes are cooked.

Easy Stroganoff

1	lb	ground beef, cooked and drained	1	16 oz pkg	egg noodles, cooked and drained
1	can	cream of chicken soup			salt and black pepper to taste
1	sm ctn	sour cream			

Brown meat and drain. Stir in cream of chicken (may substitute cream of mushroom) soup, salt and pepper. Add sour cream and stir well. Add drained noodles and mix.

Farmhouse Stew

1	lb	ground beef	8	cups	finely shredded cabbage
1	tsp	butter	1	cup	chopped onion
1	tbl	flour	1	cup	chopped green pepper
2 ½	tsp	salt	1	8-oz can	tomatoes (undrained)
1/8	tsp	pepper			

In a 12-inch skillet, saute' beef in butter until crumbly, stirring often. Mix in flour, salt and pepper. Blend in remaining ingredients and heat thoroughly. Cover and cook over low heat for 30 to 40 minutes or until cabbage is very tender

Ginger Beef

¾	cup	soy sauce	1	tbl	shortening or oil
¼	cup	water	¼	tsp	ground ginger
¼	cup	lime juice	½	tsp	minced garlic
¼	cup	brown sugar (firmly packed)	1 ½	tbl	cornstarch
2	lbs	round steak cut into 1 ½ x 1/2 –inch strips	1	lg	green pepper cut into 2-inch pieces

Blend soy sauce, water, lime juice and sugar in a large bowl. Add meat, cover and reserve marinade. Brown meat evenly in shortening or oil. Add ginger and garlic to marinade. Mix 2 tbl marinade with cornstarch to make paste. Blend paste into marinade and cook over low heat, stirring constantly until thickened. Return meat to marinade and add green pepper just before serving. Spoon over cooked fluffy rice

Home-Style Steak

½	cup	flour	1	can tomato soup
2	tbl	dry mustard		oil
1	tsp	salt	½ cup	chopped onions
	dash	pepper	1 tbl	Worcestershire sauce
2	lbs	1-inch round steak		

Combine flour, mustard, salt and pepper and sprinkle over steak. Beat with mallet or edge of saucer. Brown slowly in a little hot oil. Drain off excess oil. Combine remaining ingredients and pour over meat

Bake uncovered at 325° for 1 ½ hours or until tender. Garnish with onion rings

Hungarian Goulash

3 to 4	lbs	chuck roast cut into 1 ½-inch cubes	½ tsp	marjoram
2	tbl	oil	½ tsp	pepper
2	lg	onions sliced	2 16 oz cans	stewed tomatoes
1		green pepper chopped	1 cup	water

1		bay leaf crumbled	2	tbl	water
1	tbl	sweet Hungarian paprika	1	tbl	flour
1 ½	tsp	salt	1	cup	sour cream
1	tsp	caraway seeds			

Brown meat evenly in oil, drain and set aside. Saute' onion and green pepper in drippings until soft. Blend in seasonings and meat, tomatoes and 1 cup of water. Simmer, covered for 1 hour or until meat is tender. Mix flour with 1 to 2 tbl water and blend into goulash. Add sour cream and cook over low heat until thickened

Manicotti

CREPES:

1	cup	water
2		eggs
1	tbl	canola oil
1	cup	all-purpose flour
	dash	salt

FILLING:

1		ctn ricotta cheese
3/4	cup	mozzarella cheese shredded
3	tbl	Parmesan or Romano cheese grated
1	tbl	fresh parsley chopped
1		egg lightly beaten
1		28-oz jar spaghetti sauce
		shredded Parmesan or Romano cheese for topping

In a large bowl, combine the water, eggs and oil. Combine flour and salt; add to egg mixture and mix well. Cover and refrigerate for 1 hour.

Heat a lightly greased 8-in. nonstick skillet over medium heat; pour 2 tablespoons batter into the center of skillet. Lift and tilt pan to coat bottom evenly. Cook until top appears dry; turn and cook 15-20 seconds longer. Remove to a wire rack. Repeat with remaining batter, greasing skillet as needed. When cool, stack crepes with waxed paper or paper towels in between

For filling, combine the cheeses, parsley and egg. Spread half of spaghetti sauce in a 13-in. x 9-in. baking dish. Spoon 3 tablespoons of cheese mixture down the center of each crepe; roll up. Place seam side down over spaghetti sauce; pour remaining sauce over crepes. Sprinkle with Parmesan or Romano cheese.

Bake, uncovered, at 350° for 30 minutes or until bubbly.

Meat Noodle Casserole

1	8 oz pkg	noodles	1		sm green pepper (chopped) salt and pepper
¾	lb	ground beef			
2	sm	onions chopped	1	can	tomato soup
2	cups	celery diced	1/8	tsp	Worcestershire sauce
			½	cup	cheddar cheese grated

Cook noodles in boiling salted water, drain and rinse. Brown meat, add onion, celery and green pepper. Cook until tender. Season to taste. Alternate meat and noodles in greased casserole. Pour soup mixed with Worcestershire sauce over meat and noodles and sprinkle with cheese. Bake at 325° for about 45 minutes

Meat Pie

2	cups	all-purpose flour			milk
1/2	tsp	salt			ham, beef or chicken
2	tsp	baking powder			meat broth
2	tbl	shortening			potatoes
1		egg			

Mix together flour, salt, baking powder and shortening until crumbly. Put egg in cup; fill cup to 1/2 cup with milk. Add to dry ingredients. Mix as for pie dough and roll out thin. Cut dough into small squares and add to ham, beef or chicken broth. Bring broth to boil; reduce heat and cook over low heat until done. Add cubed potatoes and meat which was cooked to obtain broth.

Meatloaf

1½	lbs	ground beef	¼	cup	ketchup
1	cup	bread crumbs	1	tbs	salt
½	cup	milk	1	tsp	pepper
1	small	onion chopped	1		egg slightly beaten
1	tsp	cumin	1	sm can	tomato paste

Preheat oven to 350°. Combine all ingredients using only ½ of the tomato paste. Place in loaf pan (casserole dish cooks faster) and bake for 45 minutes to 1 hour. Pour off grease during cooking. Top with remaining tomato paste and sprinkle lightly with salt. Bake until meat is done.

Mini Chili Relleno Pies

1	lb	ground beef	¾	cup	milk
1		sweet onion chopped	1/8	cup	flour
2	4 oz cans	green chilies diced	2		eggs beaten
1	tsp	chili powder			additional salt and pepper
		Salt and black pepper to taste	4	tbl	taco sauce
¾	cup	pepper jack cheese, grated			Gordo's Cheese Dip heated

Brown meat with onions and drain. Add chilies, salt, pepper and chili pepper. Spray muffin tins. Divide mixture into tins. Top with cheese. Mix milk, flour, eggs, salt, pepper and taco sauce until smooth. Pour over meat mixture in tins. Bake at 375° for 15 minutes or until eggs are done. While the tin is still hot run a knife around the edge to loosen. Place on plate and sprinkle additional taco sauce around the rellenos. Pour melted cheese sauce over and around the rellenos. Serve with refried beans for a complete meal

Nob Hill Stew

2	lbs	round steak or sirloin tip, sliced thin and cut into 4-inch pieces	5	tbl	dry sherry
			1 ½	tsp	minced garlic

8	tbl	butter (melted)		1	tbl	Worcestershire sauce
		salt and pepper		1	tbl	minced parsley
1	lb	fresh whole mushrooms		2	tbl	flour
1 ½	cup	beef broth		2	tbl	water

In a large skillet, brown meat on both sides in 2 tbl butter. Season to taste. Remove meat and set aside. Add mushrooms to remaining 6 tbl butter, coat well and simmer for ten minutes. Add broth, sherry, garlic, Worcestershire sauce and parsley. Add meat, coat with sauce and continue cooking over low heat for 35 to 45 minutes. Remove meat and keep warm. Mix flour and water to make a thin paste and blend into meat sauce, stirring constantly until thickened. Add meat back to mixture 3 minutes before serving

Serve sauce over meat

Pepper Steak

4	tbl	oil		1	cup	boiling water
1	lb	cube steak, sliced in strips		2	tbl	cornstarch
1	med	onion chopped		¼	cup	water
1		garlic clove, minced		1	can	tomatoes, diced
4		bell pepper, seeded and sliced		2	tsp	soy sauce
1	cup	celery chopped				salt and black pepper to taste
2		beef bouillon cubes				

Heat oil, salt and pepper. Add meat and cook over high heat, stirring constantly until meat is browned. Add onion and garlic, green peppers and celery. Dissolve bullion cubes in boiling water and add to meat. Cover and cook over moderate heat until meat and vegetables are tender (15-20 minutes). Blend cornstarch, ¼ cup water and soy sauce and add to mixture. Cook on low heat until thickened Serve over cooked rice.

Pepper Steak And Onions

1	lb	steak cut in strips				salt and black pepper to taste
1		bell pepper seeded and sliced		4	tbl	oil for sautéing
1	med	onion sliced		3	cups	rice cooked
1	can	tomatoes diced				

Cook rice in salted water until tender. Cut steak into finger-sized strips. Best to marinate steak in soy sauce prior to cooking. Put in sauce pan with oil and saute until half-done. Add onions and bell pepper, salt and pepper to meat. Saute until tender. Add small amount of water if meat begins to stick. Add tomatoes and bring to a boil. Serve over rice

Poor Mans Steak

1-1/2	lb	lean hamburger		1	sm	onion chopped
1	tsp	salt		2	cans	cream of mushroom soup
		pepper		1	can	mushrooms drained

1/4	tsp	garlic powder		½	can	water
1	cup	bread crumbs, dry		½	can	milk
2		eggs				

Mix hamburger, salt, pepper garlic powder, bread crumbs, eggs and onion with hands.

Grease a square baking dish, form meat mixture into baking dish. Cut into 9 pieces. In large skillet, fry all pieces together in some oil, keeping pieces intact. Drain on paper towels. Return fried pieces to baking dish. Mix mushroom soup with 1/2 can water and 1/2 can milk. Pour soup over meat in baking dish. Add drained mushrooms, spread around. Bake, uncovered, at 350° for 30-40 minutes.

Porcupines

½	cup	rice		1	tsp	salt
1	lb	ground beef		1	tsp	pepper
1	tbl	onion minced		¾	cup	water
1	sm can	tomato soup				

Mix soup and water in pressure cooker. Combine rice, meat, onion, salt and pepper. Form into balls and place in tomato sauce. Cover and set "diddle" to 10. Cook 10 minutes after it begins to jiggle. Cool for 5 minutes then run cold water over lid to cool further.

Pot Roast

	3 to 4lb	beef roast (sirloin tip, rump, English cut)		2		bay leaves
1	tbl	oil		1		garlic clove, minced
1/4	cup	soy sauce		1/2	tsp	oregano
1	cup	coffee		2		onions, sliced

Sear roast in 1 tablespoon oil on all sides in heavy dutch oven. Pour sauce over meat. Put half of onions on meat, the other half in sauce. Cover and roast 4-5 hours at 325°.

Pot Roast

1	tbl	cornstarch			salt and ground pepper
8	med	carrots, cut into thirds		1	beef chuck roast (3 pounds), trimmed of excess fat
2	med	onions, chopped or cut into 8 wedges			
				2 tbl	Worcestershire sauce

In slow cooker, stir together cornstarch and 2 tablespoons cold water until smooth. Add carrots and onions; season with salt and pepper, and toss. Sprinkle roast with 1 teaspoon salt and 1/2 teaspoon pepper; place on top of vegetables, and drizzle with Worcestershire. Cover; cook on high, 6 hours (or on low 10 hours). Transfer roast to a cutting board; thinly slice against the grain. Place vegetables in a serving dish; pour pan juices through a fine-mesh sieve.

Salisbury Steak

1	can	cream of mushroom soup		1		egg beaten
1	lb	ground beef		¼	cup	onion finely chopped
¼	cup	bread crumbs		1½	cups	mushrooms sliced

In a bowl mix ¼ cup soup, beef, bread crumbs, egg and onion. Shape into ovals patties. In a skillet over high heat, cook patties until brown. Drain excess grease. Stir in remaining soup and mushrooms. Return patties to skillet. Cover and simmer 20 minutes or until done stirring occasionally.

Shepherd's Pie

beef	seasoned mashed potatoes
gravy	salt and pepper, to taste
green beans	

Mince leftover cooked beef (3 to 4 cups) and combine with beef gravy, leftover or commercially prepared. Heat through and place in a baking dish. Top with hot cooked green beans; sprinkle with salt and pepper. Top green beans with seasoned mashed potatoes; bake at 400° for 20 minutes. If desired, top with a little grated cheese just before taking it out of the oven.

Stuffed Cabbage

8		cabbage leaves (outer)				salt and black pepper to taste
1	lb	ground beef				garlic to taste
1		onion chopped		1	sm can	tomato sauce
1	cup	rice, cooked		2	tbl	brown sugar

Wash cabbage leaves (dark green leaves are usually to tough) and place in salted boiling water. Boil until tender. Remove carefully to avoid tearing. While leaves are boiling, brown meat with onion, garlic, salt and pepper. Drain and mix with cooked rice. Mix tomato sauce and brown sugar with some water. Add additional salt if needed. Bring to a boil stirring constantly. Mixture should be fairly thick. Spoon into center of cabbage leaves. Fold leaves over filling and tuck. Place in baking dish seam side down. Repeat until all leaves are filled. Pour sauce over rolls and bake at 400° for about 20 to 30 minutes. Baste during cooking.

Stuffed Peppers

4	lg	bell peppers		2	cups	rice, cooked
1	lb	ground beef				salt and freshly ground black
¼	cup	ketchup				pepper
¼	cup	Heinz 57 Steak Sauce		1	sm can	tomato sauce

Slice stem end from peppers and remove seeds. Blanch in salted hot water until medium soft. Remove from water with slotted spoon and drain water. Cook rice according to direction on package. Combine meat and onion in skillet and brown. Drain and add remaining ingredients.

Place peppers in baking dish and stuff with meat/rice mixture. Add salt to taste to tomato sauce and pour around and over peppers. Bake at 350° until peppers are soft and mixture is hot

Sunday Dinner

1	sm	roast	1	lg	onion chopped
6	lg	potatoes sliced	1	can	tomatoes diced
1	lb	carrot, peeled and diced			salt and black pepper to taste

Salt and pepper a small roast. Put in large covered baking dish. Add vegetables. Add just enough water to cover. Cover with lid or foil and back at 375° until meat is tender

Vegetable Soup

1 1/2	lbs	beef	1	lg	onion, cut up
1		soup bone	8		carrots, cut up
1	lg can	tomatoes	5		potatoes, cut up
3	stalks	celery, cut up	1	tsp	salt
1/2	cup	rice	1/2	tsp	pepper
1	tsp	sugar	1	tsp	celery seed

Cover beef and bone with water. Simmer for 1 1/2 to 2 hours. Remove bone. Add vegetables in order given: tomatoes, celery, onion, carrots and potatoes. Add spices. Continue to cook until vegetables are done.

Volcano's

1/2	lg	ground beef	1/2	can	petite diced tomatoes drained
1/2	sm	onion chopped			salt and black pepper to taste
1/	tsp	cumin	1	can	refrigerator biscuits
1/2	can	french style green beans, drained			

Brown ground beef and onion. Drain. Add cumin, salt and pepper. Stir in string beans and diced tomatoes both of which are drained. Flour surface and roll canned biscuits until flat and in a large circle. Place meat mixture in center of dough. Pull up sides to form a volcano Pinch together at the top. Brush lightly with melted butter if desired. Bake at 425° until golden brown

Yumazitti

	8-oz	egg noodles, cooked and drained			salt to taste
1½	lb	ground beef	1	10 oz can	cream of chicken soup
½	cup	celery chopped	1	10 oz can	tomato paste
2	tbs	butter	½	lb	cheddar cheese grated
¼	tsp	pepper			

Brown meat in butter, and season with salt and pepper.   Place a layer of noodles in a 2-quart casserole, then one layer each of meat, celery, soup, tomato paste and cheese. Repeat until all the ingredients are used, ending with layer of cheese and bake, uncovered, at 350° for 1 hour.

Baked Turkey Hash

2	cups	turkey, cooked and chopped	2		potatoes, boiled, peeled and diced
1	cup	celery chopped	6	slices	bacon, fried and crumbled
1		onion chopped	2	sm cans	mushrooms
½	tsp	garlic powder	½	cup	bell pepper, chopped
½	tsp	pepper	½	tsp	salt
1	cup	cheddar cheese grated			

Fry bacon crisp, drain and crumble saute celery, onion and bell pepper In bacon drippings. Add crumbled bacon, mushrooms, turkey, potatoes, garlic powder, Salt and pepper. Add a little skim milk if needed. Place in a casserole dish and bake at 350° for 15 minutes. Sprinkle with cheese and bake until cheese is melted

Bob's Baked Pork Chops & Potatoes

4		center cut pork chops	2	cans	Golden Cream of Mushroom soup
1	lg	onion chopped			olive oil
2		bell pepper, seeded and sliced			salt and pepper to taste
4	lg	potatoes sliced			

Preheat oven to 400°. Cover bottom of casserole dish with olive oil. Slice potatoes ¼ inch thick and place in bottom of dish. Slice onion into rings and cut bell peppers into strips. Place onion rings and bell pepper strips on top of potatoes. Salt and pepper pork chops and place on bottom layer and cover with onion rings. Cover with another layer of potatoes, onion rings and peppers. Pour Mushroom soup on top making sure top is completely covered. Cover dish and bake until potatoes are soft. Serve with vegetable and choice of bread

Breakfast Casserole

4	slices	bread	6		eggs beaten
12 to 16	oz	bacon or sausage, cooked and drained	2	cups	milk
2	cups	cheddar cheese shredded	1	tsp	dry mustard

Grease the bottom of a 9"x13" pan. Tear up 4 slices of bread and place in the bottom of the pan. Sprinkle cooked crumbled bacon or sausage over bread pieces. Sprinkle cheddar cheese over the bacon or sausage. Mix eggs, milk and mustard together; pour over casserole. Bake at 350° for 35 to 40 minutes.

Buttermilk Chicken

4	lg	chicken breasts		¼	tsp	pepper
1½	cups	buttermilk		¼	cup	butter, melted
¾	cup	flour		1	sm can	cream of chicken soup
1½	tsp	salt				

Dip chicken in buttermilk then roll in flour that has been seasoned with the salt and pepper. Melt butter in baking dish and place chicken—skin side down. Bake at 450° for 30 minutes. Turn chicken and bake 15 minutes. Mix remaining buttermilk with soup and blend well. Pour over chicken and bake another 15 minutes. Reduce heat to 350° and continue baking until golden brown

Buttermilk Fried Chicken

1	cup	of all-purpose flower		3 to 3 1/2	lb	fryer chicken, cut up
1	tsp	of paprika		1	cup	of buttermilk
1	tsp	of salt				vegetable oil
1/4	tsp	of pepper				

In a large bowl, mix your flour, paprika, salt and pepper. Take each piece of chicken and dip it in the buttermilk, then cover it completely in your flour mixture. Repeat the process for an added crispness. Heat the vegetable oil, to approximately 350-375, in a 12-inch skillet (oil should be 1/4 inch deep). Place chicken in heated oil and cook for 10 minutes on one side, then turn and cook for 5 minutes on the other side. The skin of the chicken should now be lightly browned on both sides. Cover the pan tightly (if the pan can not be covered tightly, add 1-2 tablespoons of water when the chicken is first placed in the pan), with a lid, and simmer for about 35 minutes, turning once or twice to ensure it is thoroughly done on both sides. The chicken is done when the juices run clear from the chicken, instead of a reddish color. Remove the cover during the last 5 minutes to increase crispness.

Cajun Stuffed Pork Chops

4		center cut pork chops		**Rub**		
1	lb	ground pork		1	tsp	salt
1/2	tsp	salt		1	tsp	cayenne pepper
1/2	tsp	cayenne pepper		1	tsp	granulated garlic
1/2	tsp	granulated garlic		1	tsp	freshly ground black pepper
1/4	tsp	freshly ground black pepper		1	tsp	paprika
1	tsp	paprika		2	cups	BBQ sauce
1/2	cup	finely chopped green onions				

On a flat surface, use a sharp knife to make a pocket inside each of the pork chops. In a mixing bowl, combine the ground pork, salt, cayenne, granulated garlic, black pepper, paprika, and green onions; mix well. Divide the pork mixture into 4 equal amounts and overstuff the mixture into the pocket of each pork chop. Mix all the rub ingredients together in a small bowl. Season each pork chop with the rub. Cover and refrigerate overnight to let the seasoning infuse into the chops. Preheat a grill or BBQ pit to 375. Put the stuffed chops on the grill or BBQ pit. After 30 minutes, turn the pork chops over. After an additional 15 minutes, turn each pork chop over and begin basting each side with BBQ sauce. Grill until a pretty glaze forms.

Chicken and Dumplings

2	quarts	water	2	cups	self rising flour
1	lg	chicken or family sized thighs	½	cup	shortening
		Salt and black pepper to taste	½	cup	chicken broth cooled

Boil chicken in salted water. Add pepper after it comes to a boil. Remove when chicken is no longer pink next to bone. Cut shortening into flour. Add cooled chicken broth. Mix until dough pulls away from sides of bowl. Roll into 1/8 inch thickness on a floured surface. Cut into strips. Drop 1 by 1 into boiling chicken broth.. Keep at a boil and stir frequently to avoid scorching. Cook until dumplings are done. Add chicken that has been cut into bite sized pieces. Add more salt and pepper as needed

Chicken and Rice

1	can	cream of chicken soup	¼	tsp	paprika
1	cup	water			salt and black pepper to taste
¾	cup	rice	4		chicken breasts -- boned and skinned

Mix soup, water, paprika and pepper and rice. Add salt as needed. Put chicken in baking dish. Pour soup mixture over chicken. Sprinkle with more paprika. Cover and bake at 375° for 45 minutes or until rice is soft and chicken is done.

Chicken and Rice Casserole

3	cups	chicken - cooked and cut up	1	can	french style green beans, drained
1	pkg	long grain wild rice, cooked	1	cup	mayonnaise
1	can	cream of mushroom soup, no water added	1	can	water chestnuts, sliced
					salt and black pepper to taste
1	sm jar	pimento, chopped			
1	med	onion chopped			

Mix all ingredients and pour into greased casserole dish. Bake at 350° for 25 to 30 minutes

Chicken Asparagus Casserole

2	cans	asparagus drained	1	tbl	lemon juice
4		chicken breast halves, cooked and chopped	1	cup	cheddar cheese shredded
			1	cup	bread crumbs
2	cans	cream of chicken soup			
3/4	cup	mayonnaise			

Layer asparagus in buttered 9 x 13 x 2-inch baking pan; top with chicken. Mix soup, mayonnaise, and lemon juice; pour over chicken and asparagus. Top with cheese and bread crumbs. Bake at 350° for 30 to 40 minutes

Chicken Casserole

4 to 6		chicken breasts	1	8 oz	package Pepperidge Farm Cornbread Stuffing
1	can	cream of mushroom soup			
1	can	cream of chicken soup	3	cups	chicken broth, reserved from boiling chicken
			1		stick margarine

Boil chicken, de-bone, and tear into pieces. Place chicken into a 13×9 casserole dish.
Mix Cream of Chicken soup with 1-and-a-half cups of chicken broth. Pour over chicken.
Mix Cream of Mushroom soup with 1-and-a-half cups of chicken broth. Pour over chicken.
Melt one stick of margarine and mix with stuffing. Spoon on top of chicken/soup. Cover with foil and bake 30 minutes at 350° . Remove foil and bake for another 7-10 minutes, until brown and bubbly.

Chicken Creole

		non-stick spray coating	1/4	cup	chopped onion
4		med chicken breast, skinned, boned, halved and cut into 1-inch strips	2	cloves	garlic, minced
			1	tbl	chopped fresh basil
			1	tbl	chopped fresh parsley
1		can tomatoes diced	1/4	tsp	salt
1-1/2	cups	chopped green pepper	¼	tsp	crushed red pepper
1	cup	chili sauce			cooked rice
1/2	cup	chopped celery			

Coat deep skillet with a light coat of cooking spray. Over medium-high heat cook and stir raw chicken for 5 to 10 minutes or until chicken is no longer pink. Reduce heat then add diced tomatoes with juice, green peppers, chili sauce, celery, onion, garlic, basil, parsley, salt and red pepper. Bring chicken creole to a boil, reduce heat and simmer covered for about 10 minutes. Serve over steaming hot rice.

Chicken Rolls

1	can	crescent rolls	½	cup	milk
1	can	cream of chicken soup	½	cup	cheddar cheese grated
3		chicken breasts			

Boil chicken until done and cut into pieces. Mix soup, milk and cheese together. Coat baking dish with non-stick spray. Roll out rolls and place chicken inside rolls and roll it up with ends closed. Top with soup mixture. Cook uncovered at 450° for 35 to 45 minutes

Chicken Turnovers

1	6 oz pkg	cream cheese		2	tbl	onion chopped
5	tbl	butter, melted and divided		1	tbl	pimento, chopped
4	cups	chicken, cooked and chopped		2	cans	crescent rolls
¼	cup	milk		¾	cup	Italian bread crumbs
		salt and black pepper to taste				

Blend cream cheese & 3 tablespoon butter. Add chicken, milk, salt, black pepper, onion and pimento and fold together until blended. Unroll crescent roll dough and divide into rectangles (4 per can) pressing together the diagonal perforations. Place rounded 1/2 cup chicken mixture in center of each dough rectangle. Fold dough over filling and pressing edges together to seal. Dip turnovers in remaining melted butter and then roll in bread crumbs. Bake at 350° degrees for about 15-20 minutes or until golden brown. These can be assembled ahead of time and then placed in the oven 30 minutes before serving. If you find it difficult for the perforations to "hold together" you may want to try using a rolling pin to gently roll the perforations together

Company Chicken and Broccoli

2	lg pkgs	frozen broccoli		3	tbl	lemon juice
1	lg pkg	chicken breasts		1	cup	mayonnaise
2	cans	cream of chicken soup		1	8-oz pkg	sharp cheddar cheese grated

Boil chicken until done. Boil and drain broccoli. Line chicken in large baking dish placing broccoli around chicken. Mix soup, mayonnaise and lemon juice together and pour over chicken and broccoli. Top with grated cheese. Bake at 350° until bubbly and cheese is melted.

Easy Chicken Pie

5		chicken breasts		1	sm can	cream of chicken soup
5		eggs, boiled and chopped		1	cup	self rising flour
2¼	cups	chicken broth		1	stick	butter (no substitutes), melted

Boil and debone chicken and cut into pieces. Spray large dish with non-stick spray and add chicken. Slice eggs and put over chicken. Salt and pepper to taste. Mix broth with soup and pour over meat. Mix flour and butter then add milk and mix well. Pour over other ingredients in dish. Bake at 350° for 1 hour or until crust comes to the top and browns.

Fried Green Tomato BLT With Remoulade Sauce

Note: I use Organic or Romaine instead of Iceberg lettuce

BLT

		bacon slices
1	lg	green tomato thinly sliced
		lettuce leaves
		Batter

Remoulade Sauce

1	cup	mayonnaise
1	tsp	lemon juice
2	tsp	parsley minced
2	tsp	spicy brown or dijon mustard

2	cups	self rising flour		2	tbl	relish
2	tbl	cajun seasoning		½	cup	ketchup
1	tsp	salt		1	tsp	horseradish
		milk to form batter		1	tbl	cajun seasoning or to taste

Whisk together mayonnaise, lemon juice, parsley, mustard, relish, ketchup, horseradish and cajun seasoning and chill. Fry slices of a good quality bacon and drain on paper towel. Thinly slice one large green tomato. Make a batter of 2 cups self-rising flour, 2 tablespoons Cajun seasoning and 1-teaspoon salt. Add milk until batter begins to thin but will coat the tomato slices. Coat sliced tomatoes with batter and drop into hot grease. Turn frequently to avoid burning. Toast slices of French or Italian bread. When bacon and tomato slices are all cooked, stack them on the toasted bread with lettuce and add the Remoulade Sauce.

Honey Mustard Pork Tenderloin

2		pork tenderloins, about 1 pound each		2	tbl	brown sugar
		salt and pepper		1	tbl	cider vinegar or balsamic vinegar
1	sm	clove garlic, minced		1/2	tsp	dried leaf thyme, crumbled
4	tbl	Dijon mustard		1	tbl	cornstarch
2	tbl	honey		1	tbl	cold water

Wash and trim the pork and pat dry; sprinkle lightly with salt and pepper. Place pork in the slow cooker. Combine garlic, mustard, honey, brown sugar, vinegar, and thyme; pour over the pork. Turn pork to coat thoroughly. Cover and cook on LOW for 7 to 9 hours, or on HIGH for 3 1/2 to 4 1/2 hours.

Remove pork to a plate, cover with foil, and keep warm. Pour the juices into a saucepan and bring to a boil over medium heat. Simmer for 8 to 10 minutes, or until reduced by about one-third. Combine the cornstarch and cold water; whisk into the reduced juices and cook for 1 minute longer. Serve pork sliced with the thickened juices.

One Dish Meal

6		pork chops,	1	can	white peas
1		onion sliced	1	can (6 oz)	tomato paste
1	tsp	garlic salt	1	can	butter beans
		salt and black pepper to taste	1	can	mushrooms
4	lg	potatos peeled and sliced	1	can	tomatoes diced
1	can	english peas			

Sean chops with salt, pepper and garlic powder. Brown on both sides. Place in bottom of large baking dish. Layer vegetables. Add a little water if needed. Cover and bake at 350° until potatoes are tender

Oven BBQ Chicken

3	lb	chicken	1	tsp	dried mustard

3/4 cup	chili sauce	1/2 tsp	prepared horseradish
2 tbl	of honey	½ tsp	red pepper sauce
2 tbl	soy sauce		

Preheat your oven to 375°. Place chicken, skin up, in an ungreased rectangular pan. Mix all of your remaining ingredients in a small bowl. Pour the entire contents of the bowl over your chicken, spreading the sauce evenly over the chicken. Cover the pan, with the chicken in it, with aluminum foil tightly. Bake it for approximately 30 minutes, then remove the foil and spoon sauce over the chicken. Bake uncovered for another 30 minutes or until the juices run clear.

Pork and Sweet Potato Stew

1/3 cup	brown sugar	2	garlic cloves minced
1/3 cup	flour	1 1/3 cups	chicken broth
1/4 cup	Dijon mustard	1 cup	dry sherry
3 lbs	pork, cut in 1 inch cubes	3 lbs	sweet potatoes, peeled and cut in 1 inch cubes
3 tbl	olive oil		salt and pepper
1	onion chopped	1/4 cup	parsley chopped

Preheat oven to 350°. Combine brown sugar and flour in a small bowl. Coat pork cubes in mustard, then in the flour mixture. Heat oil in a large frying pan, and brown pork cubes on all sides. Transfer pork cubes to a large casserole dish. Continue until all pork cubes are browned. Add onions and garlic to the frying pan and cook until softened but not brown then to the casserole dish.

Discard any fat in the frying pan. Add the broth and sherry to the pan, and bring to a boil. Pour into the casserole dish. Add sweet potato cubes to the casserole dish. Cover and bake for 50 to 60 minutes, until meat and sweet potatoes are tender. Season with salt and pepper to taste, and add parsley.

Pork Chop And Rice Casserole

6	pork chops	1/2 cup	bell peppers, chopped
2 cups	rice, uncooked	2/3 cup	onions, chopped
4 cups	tomato juice		

Wash pork chops; dry. Add salt and pepper and coat with flour. Fry chops in oil until brown. Place in casserole dish. Pour 2 cups rice over chops, sprinkle bell peppers and onions over rice. Pour 4 cups tomato juice over top of peppers and onions. Cover with foil. Bake at 350° until rice is fluffy and tender.

Pork Chops With Beer And Bacon Gravy

4	bone-in pork chops	1 tbl	all-purpose flour
1 tbl	extra-virgin olive oil, plus a drizzle	1 bottle	amber to dark German beer
2 slices	smoky bacon diced	1/2 cup	stock

| 1 | | med onion, diced | | | parsley, chopped |

Season the chops liberally with salt and pepper. Heat the extra-virgin olive oil in a skillet over medium-high heat. When the oil smokes, add the chops and cook, turning once, until caramelized and the meat is just turning firm, about 10 to 12 minutes. Remove to a platter and cover with foil, reserve.

Add a drizzle more oil to the pan, add bacon and brown for 2 to 3 minutes. Stir in the onions and saute over medium heat with the bacon until soft, 6 to 7 minutes. Sprinkle in flour, stir for 1 minute, then add the beer. Cook until reduced by half, 1 to 2 minutes more, then whisk in the stock. Remove from the heat and season with pepper. Pour the gravy over the chops, sprinkle with parsley and serve immediately.

Pork Chops With Corn Dressing

1		egg, beaten	1	tsp	Worcestershire sauce
2	cups	soft bread crumbs	2	tbl	vegetable oil
1	can	whole kernel corn, drained	6		butterfly pork chops (about 1 inch thick)
1/4	cup	water			
1/2	cup	chopped green pepper			salt and pepper to taste
1	sm	onion, chopped	1	can	cream of mushroom soup, undiluted
			2/3	cup	milk

In a bowl, combine the egg, bread crumbs, corn, water, green pepper, onion and Worcestershire sauce; set aside. In a large ovenproof skillet or a dutch oven, heat oil over medium heat. Lightly brown pork chops on both sides. Season with salt and pepper. Top with corn dressing mixture. Add enough water to cover bottom of pan.

Bake, uncovered, at 350° for about 1 hour or until pork is tender. Add additional water to pan if necessary. Remove pork chops and dressing to a serving platter; keep warm. Skim fat from drippings. Add soup and milk to pan drippings. Cook and stir over medium heat until hot and bubbly. Serve with pork chops.

Ranch Style Casserole

1		package onion soup mix	1	lb	chicken breast halves, deboned and skinned
1	tbl	all-purpose flour			
1/2	cup	milk	2	cups	frozen mixed vegetables
1		sm ctn sour cream	1/4	cup	bread crumbs
2		garlic cloves, finely chopped	1	tbl	butter
2	tsp	lemon juice	2	cups	rice cooked

Preheat oven to 350°. Add onion soup mix, all purpose flour, sour cream, milk, garlic, and fresh lemon juice to medium mixing bowl. Stir to combine. Place chicken breasts in single layer in casserole dish. Spoon soup mixture over chicken. Cover and bake 20 minutes. Remove cover; sprinkle chicken casserole with bread crumbs and dot with butter. Continue baking, uncovered, 25 minutes.

Serve with hot cooked rice.

Southern Ham Casserole

2	cups	ham, cooked	1	cup	cheddar cheese shredded
1	cup	creamed corn	2	tbs	onion minced
1	tsp	worcestershire sauce	¼	cup	milk
1		egg	2/3	cup	biscuit mix
1	cup	lima beans, drained			

Mix ham, beans, corn, cheese, onion and Worcestershire sauce. Pour into greased casserole. Bake covered at 375° for 15 minutes. Mix remaining ingredients and spread evenly over casserole. Bake uncovered for 15 to 20 minutes.

Southern Style Chicken and Dumplings

3	lbs	whole chicken	1/2	tsp	dried thyme
1		onion, quartered	2	cups	all-purpose flour
2	slices	lemon	3	tbl	shortening
		salt and pepper to taste	1	tsp	salt
3	cups	water	1/4	cup	water
1		bay leaf			

In a heavy pot with a lid place the chicken, onion, lemon, salt, pepper, water, bay leaf and thyme. Simmer all over low heat until tender, about 1 hour.

Let chicken cool slightly in pot, then remove and take the meat off of the bones. Discard the bones and skin and skim excess fat off the broth if desired. Discard the onion, lemon and bay leaf. If desired, wash out pot well. Return broth and chicken pieces to the pot. Simmer over low heat while making the dumplings.

To Make Dumplings: In a medium mixing bowl, cut shortening into the flour and salt. Stir in 1/4 cup water (more if needed) to form a soft dough. Roll out dough on a floured surface, with a rolling pin, until very thin. Cut into 1 inch wide strips using a pizza cutter or knife. Tear off 1 inch long pieces from these strips and drop into simmering broth and chicken meat. Simmer for 10 minutes with the lid off, then 10 minutes more with the lid on. Serve immediately.

Special Chicken

1	cup	rice	12		chicken breast fillets
1	stick	margarine		4 oz	thinly sliced ham
2	cans	chicken broth		4 oz	swiss cheese slices

Brown rice in margarine in heavy skillet. Stir in chicken broth. Pour into 2 quart casserole dish. Place chicken in rice mixture. Bake at 350 for 1 hour. Layer ham slices and cheese over chicken. Bake until cheese melts

Stuffed Pork Chops

1/2	cup	salt	1	tbl	freshly chopped rosemary leaves

1	tbl	light brown sugar		1	tbl	freshly chopped sage leaves
2	quarts	water		2	tbl	freshly chopped parsley leaves
4		pork chops, bone-in rib loin chops, split to bone		2 1/2	cups	crumbled cornbread
				1/4	cup	dried cranberries
2	slices	bacon, chopped		1/2	cup	chicken broth
2	stalks	elery, minced				salt and freshly ground black pepper
1	sm	onion, minced				
2		cloves garlic, minced				

Whisk salt and sugars in 2-quarts of cold water. Add pork chops and cover. Refrigerate for 1 hour. Remove the pork chops from the brine and dry well. In a large heavy bottomed saute pan, begin to fry bacon. Add celery, onion and garlic to pan and allow to saute with the crispy bacon. Add rosemary, sage and parsley after bacon has cooked for 8 to 10 minutes. Saute until fragrant. Season with salt and pepper. In a large bowl add cornbread, dried cranberries and chicken stock. Stir in the cooked vegetable mixture. Mix well.

Preheat grill to medium-high heat.

Season the pork chops with salt and pepper. Stuff the chop with about 1/2 cup of stuffing. Use toothpicks to help seal the chops. Grill the chops for 5 to 7 minutes per side. Allow chop to rest for 5 minutes before serving.

Turkey Pot Pie

Filling

3	cups	turkey, cooked and chopped
1	can	english peas, drained
1	can	carrots
1	med	onion chopped
3		eggs, boiled and chopped
2	sm cans	cream of chicken soup, no water added

1	sm can	cream of mushroom soup, no water added

Crust

1	cup	plain flour
1	cup	milk
¾	cup	mayonnaise

Mix all filling ingredients together. Pour into large baking dish. Mix crust ingredients together and spread evenly over filling. Bake at 350° degrees for 1 hour or until brown

Seafood

Baked Fish with Lemon-Pepper Crust

1	cup	bread crumbs		24 oz	fish fillets
¼	cup	parsley minced		2	tbl	butter melted
1	tsp	lemon pepper		2		lemons juiced
½	tsp	salt				

Preheat oven to 450°. In a bowl, combine bread crumbs, parsley, pepper and salt. Set aside. Dip fish into melted butter and coat both sides with crumb mixture. Place on a baking sheet and bake until cooked through yet flaky to the fork, about 10 minutes. Sprinkle with lemon juice and serve.

Beer-Battered Fish

1	lb	fish fillets		1/2	cup	beer
3 to 4	tbl	biscuit mix		1		egg
1	cup	biscuit mix		1/2	tsp	salt

Heat oil in deep fryer. Lightly coat fish with 3 to 4 tablespoons biscuit mix. Mix remaining ingredients with hand beater until smooth. Dip fish into batter, letting excess drip into bowl. Fry fish about 4 minutes or until golden brown; drain. Serve hot with tartar sauce.

Blackened Catfish

6 to 8		catfish fillets, thinly sliced		1/2	tsp	garlic powder
1	tsp	crushed dried thyme leaves		1/2	tsp	onion powder
1	tsp	cayenne pepper		1/2	tsp	paprika
1	tsp	black pepper		1/2	cup	butter, melted
1	tsp	salt				lemon juice

Rinse catfish fillets under running cold and then thoroughly pat dry with paper towels.

Make your seasoning mixture by combining crushed dried thyme leaves, cayenne pepper, black pepper, salt, garlic powder, onion powder and paprika in a small bowl. Brush melted butter lightly over catfish fillets and sprinkle with blackened seasoning mix. Repeat for other side. Be sure to completely coat each fillet. Heat iron cast skillet until it is very hot, about 10 minutes. Pour the leftover butter into your skillet. Carefully place the catfish fillets into the skillet and cook for about 4 minutes on both sides. This blackened seasoning mixture will produce some smoke so another way to tell when to turn over you fillets is when the smoke turns gray.

Bob's Crispy Fish Fillets

6		fish fillets	2	tbl	mayonnaise
1	cup	cornmeal			salt

Heat oil on medium heat. Add enough water to corn meal to make a thick paste. Add mayonnaise and mix well. Sprinkle fillets with salt and dip onto corn meal and mayonnaise mixture. Cook until golden brown

Broiled Salmon

2		pieces fresh salmon		lemon juice
3	tbl	butter		salt and black pepper to taste

Remove skin from back of salmon. Remove any bones. Place salmon on broiler pan sprayed with non-stick spray. Salt and pepper to taste. Dot with soft butter. Sprinkle lemon juice over salmon. Broil until butter is melted and salmon is flaky. DO NOT OVER COOK

Cajun Baked Catfish

2	tbl	canola oil	1/2	tsp	cayenne pepper
2	tsp	garlic salt	1/2	tsp	hot pepper sauce
2	tsp	dried thyme	1/4	tsp	pepper
2	tsp	paprika	4		8oz fillets catfish

In a small bowl, combine the first seven ingredients brush over both sides of fish. Place fish in a 13-in. x 9-in. x 2-in. baking dish coated with nonstick cooking spray. Bake at 450 for 10-13 minutes or until fish flakes easily with a fork.

Cajun-Style Sauted Fish

1	lb	tuna steak, or other firm fish	1	tbl	minced peeled onion
1	tsp	paprika	1/2	tsp	minced garlic
1/4	tsp	ground black pepper	1		lemon, juiced
1/4	tsp	ground cumin	1	tbl	white distilled vinegar
1/4	tsp	cayenne pepper	1/8	tsp	salt
1/4	tsp	crushed dried thyme	2	tbl	parsley chopped
1/4	tsp	crushed dried oregano	1		lime, cut into wedges
1/4	tsp	crushed dried basil			

Rinse fish, drain and set aside. In a small bowl, combine paprika, pepper, cumin, cayenne, thyme, oregano and basil. Heat a 10-inch nonstick pan or skillet on medium heat. Add spice mixture and toast, stirring constantly, for 30 to 50 seconds or until fragrant. Add onion and garlic and cook, stirring constantly for 1 minute. Add fish, lemon juice, vinegar and salt. Cover, reduce heat to low, and cook 3 minutes. Turn fish over and cook for another 5 minutes or until fish is tender. Raise heat to reduce some of the liquid. Transfer to a serving plate and spoon on spicy juices. Serve with parsley and lime wedges.

Crab and Mushroom Ravioli with Corn-Lemon Sauce

1	tbl	butter
	8 oz	shiitake or white mushrooms, coarsely chopped
1		garlic clove, finely minced
1/2	lb	picked crab leg meat, coarsely chopped
1/2	cup	frozen corn kernels, thawed
1/4	cup	sour cream
2	tbl	finely chopped green onions
		zest of 1 lemon
		salt and black pepper to taste
1		package square wonton skins
		Egg wash (1 egg mixed with 3 tablespoons water)

Lemon-Corn Sauce

		green onions, sliced
		Corn-Lemon Sauce
1	tbl	vegetable oil
1		medium onion, coarsely chopped
1 1/2	tsp	minced ginger root
2	cups	frozen corn kernels, thawed
2	cups	chicken broth
2	tbl	butter
		juice of 2 large lemons
		salt and black pepper to taste

Saute mushrooms and garlic in butter over medium heat until mushrooms are tender, about 5 minutes. Remove from heat and allow mixture to cool. In a bowl, combine the mushroom mixture with the crab, corn, sour cream, green onions and lemon zest. Season with salt and pepper. Lay out 4 wonton skins at a time and place 1 tablespoon of mix in the center of each. Brush egg wash around the edges and place second wonton skin on top. Press down firmly to seal edges. Repeat with remaining ingredients. Once raviolis are assembled, cook for 2 minutes in a large pot of boiling, salted water. Remove and drain raviolis well. To serve, ladle Corn-Lemon Sauce into individual shallow soup bowls, place raviolis on the sauce and garnish with green onions.

To make sauce: In a saucepan heat oil over medium-high heat and saute onions and ginger until onions have softened, about 4 minutes. Add the corn and cook, stirring frequently, for 2 minutes. Add the broth, bring to a simmer and cook, uncovered, for 15 minutes. Puree the sauce using a blender (or hand blender) to make a smooth puree. Return pureed sauce to pan and reheat just to a boil. Remove from heat and stir in the butter and lemon juice. Season to taste with salt and pepper.

Crispy Fish Fillets

choice of fish	3 eggs
corn flakes	salt

Heat oil on medium heat. Crumble corn flakes (fine). Beat eggs (well). Sprinkle fillets with salt. Dip fillets into eggs then onto corn flake. Cook until golden brown. Turn with slotted spoon or spatula to prevent breaking

Fried Crawfish Tails

	vegetable oil for deep frying		dash	white vinegar
1	lb	peeled crawfish tails	1/4 cup	water

	salt to taste		1	tsp	baking powder
	cayenne to taste		1/4	cup	all-purpose
1	lg egg		1/4	cup	Italian-style bread crumbs

Heat 4 inches of the oil in a deep fryer. Season the crawfish with salt and cayenne. In a small bowl beat the egg and add the vinegar, water, baking powder, and mix well. Add the crawfish tails. In another bowl, combine the flour and bread crumbs, and season with salt and cayenne. Drain the crawfish tails, and then toss them in the flour and bread crumb mixture. Shake off excess. Drop the tails, a few at a time, into the hot oil and fry until golden brown. Drain on paper towels.

Grilled Fish

1/4	cup	soy sauce	1		slice ginger root, 1-inch long, halved
1		green onion, coarsely chopped	4		6-oz fish fillets
1/2		lemon, sliced			

Combine soy sauce, onion, lemon, ginger, and fish fillets in a ziplock bag. Marinate in the refrigerator for 30 minutes, turning periodically. Prepare hot coals in the grill (or preheat gas grill). Spray grill rack with nonstick cooking spray. Heat a well-greased grill to medium-high heat. Remove fillets from bag, discarding marinade and place on the grill. Cook about 4 to 5 minutes per side, turning once or until fish is firm and flaky.

Oyster Casserole

2	quarts	oysters	1	cup	heavy cream
1	stick	butter	¼	cup	Parmesan cheese grated
3		green onion chopped	1/8	tsp	nutmeg
1		bell pepper, chopped	½	tsp	paprika
½	lb	mushrooms sliced	½	cup	bread crumbs
¼	cup	flour			Salt and black pepper to taste

Preheat the broiler. Grease a 9x13-inch ovenproof serving dish or spray it with nonstick spray. Drain the oysters and set aside. Melt 2 tablespoons of the butter in a heavy casserole. Add the scallions and pepper and sauté until the onion is soft, about 5 minutes. Add the mushrooms and oysters and sauté for 5 minutes. In a separate pan, melt 2 tablespoons of the remaining butter. Stir in the flour. When smooth, add the cream, and stir until boiling and thick. Add the cheese. Stir this cheese sauce into the oyster mixture and season with nutmeg, paprika, salt, and pepper. The casserole may be made ahead to this point and refrigerated overnight. Return it to the simmer on top of the stove before proceeding. Pour the mixture into the prepared dish and top with the bread crumbs and dot with the remaining butter. Place under the broiler until browned and bubbling—about 10 minutes, depending on the depth of the casserole.

Salmon Patties

1	can	salmon, drained, fine bones removed	½	cup	flour
		salt and black pepper to taste			additional flour to coat patties

| 1 | onion chopped | | 1 | egg |

Mix all ingredients and shape into patties. Coat with flour. Heat oil in cast iron skillet. Add patties and fry until light brown on each side. Drain and serve hot

Shrimp Jambalaya

1	cup	sliced celery	1 ½	tsp	salt
2	cups	diced green pepper	¼	tsp	hot pepper sauce
2		med onions thinly sliced	½	tsp	chili powder
4	tbl	butter or margarine	1	tsp	sugar
1		garlic clove minced	2	16-oz cans	whole tomatoes
1	lb	cooked ham cubed	3	cups	hot cooked rice
2	lbs	peeled shrimp divided			

Cook celery, green pepper and onion in half the butter or margarine until tender but not brown. Add garlic and ham, cook 5 minutes longer. Add remaining butter, shrimp, salt, hot pepper sauce, chili powder and sugar. Cook tossing often with fork until shrimp is pink. Add tomatoes and heat then stir in rice

Shrimp With Tarragon Aïoli

3/4	cup	mayonnaise			kosher salt and black pepper
1/2	cup	dill pickles, finely chopped	1 1/4	lbs	cooked peeled and deveined large shrimp
2	tbl	fresh tarragon, chopped	1	cup	store-bought cocktail sauce

In a small bowl, combine the mayonnaise, pickles, tarragon, and ¼ teaspoon each salt and pepper. Serve with the shrimp and cocktail sauce.

Southern Fried Fish

	fish		yellow cornmeal
	salt and pepper to taste		flour
	peanut oil		

Clean the fish and season with salt and lots of black pepper, use garlic powder if you must. Heat fresh corn oil or peanut oil in a cast iron skillet. There should be at least 1 inch of hot oil. Coat fish with a combination of yellow cornmeal and flour, 3 parts corn meal to 1 part flour. Shake off any excess coating. Lay fish into hot oil and don't move it until ready to turn... Add other pieces to the pan but don't crowd. When fish are brown around the edges, it is ready to turn, usually about 5 minutes in hot oil over medium high heat. Turn fish with a slotted spatula to avoid breaking. Fish should be golden brown on both sides crusty on the outside and moist and flaky on the inside.

Wild Rice and Oysters

4	cups	uncooked wild rice
2	pint	fresh oysters
1	cup	parmesan cheese

Sauce

1		box fresh or frozen mushrooms
1	cup	combined minced onion, celery and green pepper
1	pint	heavy cream

2	tbl	curry
1 ½		sticks butter (do not substitute with oleo)
6	tbl	flour
2		cans mushroom soup
		salt and pepper taste

Prepare wild rice as directed on package and drain.

To make sauce: Slice and sauté mushrooms in 2 tbl butter. Remove and add 2 tbl butter and sauté onion, celery and green pepper. In a sauce pan, melt remaining stick of butter, blend in flour. Stir in cream, soup and seasonings. Slowly add sauted vegetables. In a 3 quart casserole, put layers of rice, half of sauce and oysters. Repeat once. You may top with one cup grated parmesan cheese, if desired.

Bake uncovered ½ hour at 375°

Wild Game & Birds

Baked Doves In Wild Rice

		dove breasts	1	can	milk
1	box	wild rice	1	can	water
1	can	cream of chicken soup	1	sm	onion chopped
1	can	cream of celery soup			salt and black pepper to taste

Clean birds. Mix all ingredients in casserole pan and lay dove breasts on top of mixture. Cover with aluminum foil and bake 2 to 2 1/2 hours at 325°

BARBECUED VENISON

		deer meat	1 1/2	cups	water
1		envelope onion soup mix,	1/2	cup	butter
1/2	cup	vinegar	1	tsp	pepper
1/4	cup	sugar,	1	cup	ketchup
2	tsp	salt			

Remove all fat. Cook deer meat until well done. Remove meat from bones and cut up. Pour barbecue sauce over meat and put in oven to heat. This is a good way to use the bony parts of a deer. Freezes nicely.

Sauce: combine onion soup mix, vinegar, sugar, salt, water, butter and 1 tsp. pepper. Simmer 10 minutes. Add ketchup. Stir and heat.

BBQ Venison

1	envelope	onion soup mix	1½	cups	water
½	cup	vinegar	½	cup	butter
¼	cup	sugar	1	tsp	pepper
2	tsp	salt	1	cup	ketchup

Remove all fat. Cook deer meat until well done. Remove meat from bones and cut up. Pour barbecue sauce over meat and put in oven to heat. This is a good way to use the bony parts of a deer. Freezes nicely. Sauce: combine onion soup mix, vinegar, sugar, water, butter , and pepper. Simmer 10 minutes. Add ketchup. Stir and heat. Makes 1 quart.

Braised Pheasant

1		pheasant, cleaned and quartered	2 oz		brandy or rum extract
1	med	onion chopped	½	cup	white wine or sherry
2	stalks	celery chopped	1	tbl	sweet cream

1   tsp   cornstarch

Make a broth using pheasant neck, wings, liver, and back by covering pieces with water, add onion and celery, and cook until meat can be easily removed from bones. Remove bones and return meat to broth. Thicken with cornstarch. Salt and pepper to taste. Brush pheasant with butter; place in a skillet and brown, or place in a pan and brown under broiler. Add warm brandy to skillet or pan with pheasant and ignite brandy. Remove bird and put in pan just large enough to hold it. Add broth to the pan used to brown bird and let it simmer 2-3 minutes. Add wine to broth and pour over bird, nearly covering the meat. If there isn't enough broth, add some chicken broth. Bake at 325° until bird is tender. Optional: drizzle another 1/2 cup wine through the sauce. When done, add sweet cream. Place bird on platter and pour sauce over meat.

Brown Venison Stew

1	lb	venison, cubed	3	lg	potatoes sliced
		flour	2		onion chopped
		salt and black pepper to taste	3		carrots peeled and diced
3	tbs	oil	1	cup	snap beans
1½	cups	water			

Roll meat cubes in flour that has been salted and peppered. Brown in oil. Add water and cover. Simmer 2 to 3 hours or until almost tender. Add vegetables and continue simmering covered until all are tender.

Crispy Frog Legs

5	lbs	small frog legs	2	tbl	olive or vegetable oil
¾	cup	lemon juice or vinegar			salt and freshly ground black pepper
		crushed ice	1½	cups	flour
1	cup	milk	¼	tsp	salt
6		eggs separated			vegetable oil

Wash frog legs thoroughly. Place in a large Dutch oven; sprinkle with lemon juice, and cover with crushed ice. Refrigerate 1 to 3 hours. Combine milk, egg yolks, olive oil, and 1/4 tsp. salt; mix well. Beat egg whites until stiff; fold into batter. Sprinkle frog legs with salt and pepper; dip each in batter, and dredge in flour. Fry until golden brown in deep oil heated to 375°. Drain on paper towels

Duck Stew

2		dressed duck cut in serving pieces	3	bunches	green onion chopped
		Red pepper to taste			salt and black pepper to taste
		garlic to taste	4	lg	onion chopped
1 to 2	pints	water	1		bell pepper, chopped
½	cup	oil			Parsley -- chopped

3   stalks   celery chopped

Season duck with salt, black pepper, and red pepper. Heat oil in large, heavy pan until very hot. Brown ducks in hot oil. Remove from pan; place onions, garlic, celery, and green pepper in same pan. Replace duck in pan. Cook over medium heat for 15 minutes, stirring frequently. Add water; cover. Cook slowly for 2 1/2 hours or until tender. Replenish water if necessary. About 15 minutes before serving, add green onions and parsley. Serve over rice, if desired.

Easy Rabbit Stew

1		frozen dressed rabbit		3	tbl	catsup or tomato paste
1	lg	onion chopped				cayenne pepper to taste
1	sm	bell pepper, chopped		1	cup	liquid (white wine, cider, tomato sauce, or water)
1 or 2	stalks	celery chopped				
2	cloves	garlic, chopped		**Marinade:**		
		salt and pepper		1/2	cup	vinegar
1/2	tsp	oregano		2	tbl	salt
1	tbl	dried parsley		2	cloves	garlic minced
1 or 2		carrots sliced				cold water to cover

Defrost rabbit meat overnight in marinade. Brown rabbit with vegetables in hot skillet for 5-10 minutes. Place rabbit and other ingredients in crock pot. Cover and cook on low 8-10 hours.

Easy Venison Sausage

5	lbs	lean venison	1	tbl	salt
1	tbs	rubbed sage	1	tbl	liquid smoke
1		med square of cured bacon			

Grind and thoroughly mix all ingredients, form into patties and pan fry. Keeps 2-3 months in the freezer.

Fried Goose Breasts

1	pair	goose breasts	1/4	cup	bacon fat
1/4	cup	flour			milk
		salt and pepper to taste			

Skin the goose and slice out the whole breasts. Slice about 1/4 inch thick, across the grain. Dredge in seasoned flour, and pound, to tenderize. Fry in hot fat for 1 minute on each side. Remove the meat from the pan and stir in 1 tbl. flour for each 1 tbl fat remaining. When smooth, stir in milk to make gravy of the right consistency. Add salt, pepper, or other condiments to the gravy, and pour it over the fried goose breasts.

Frog Legs

5	lbs	small frog legs	2	tbl	oil	
¾	cup	lemon juice	¼	tsp	salt	
		crushed ice			salt and pepper to taste	
1	cup	milk	1½	cup	flour	
6		eggs separated			Oil for frying	

Wash frog legs thoroughly. Place in a large Dutch oven; sprinkle with lemon juice, and cover with crushed ice. Refrigerate 1 to 3 hours. Combine milk, egg yolks, olive oil, and 1/4 tsp. salt; mix well. Beat egg whites until stiff; fold into batter. Sprinkle frog legs with salt and pepper; dip each in batter, and dredge in flour. Fry until golden brown in deep oil. Drain on paper towels.

Heavenly Quail

1	pint	milk	1	small	onion chopped
¼	lb	butter	1	tbs	salt
2	stalks	celery chopped	1	tsp	pepper
1	cup	sherry	1	doz	quail

Mix all ingredients and pour over quail. Cover and simmer for 2 hours at 325°. Add more milk if needed

Oxtail Soup

		fresh or frozen oxtails	1	can	diced tomatoes
	sm bag	mixed vegetables (fresh or frozen)			salt and pepper to taste
1	can	tomato sauce			

Start off by boiling your oxtails over medium-low heat until they are tender. Spoon away any foam that forms as the oxtails boils. Once oxtails are tender add the mixed vegetables, tomato sauce and diced tomatoes plus salt and pepper to taste. Reduce heat to a simmer and continue to cook for about 1 hour.

Oxtails With Buttered Rice

6 to 8	thin	oxtail slices	2	lg	sweet onions sliced
		salt and pepper to taste	1	tbl	Old Bay Seasoning
		garlic powder to taste	4	cups	cooked rice buttered
4	tbl	soy sauce			

Preheat oven to 350° Remove excess fat from oxtails. Put ox tails in large casserole dish. Sprinkle with salt, pepper and garlic powder. Mix soy sauce and Old Bay and pour over ox tails. Add onions. Pour about 1 cup water into dish making sure bottom of dish is covered..   Cover and bake until oxtails are tender, removing foil last 10 minutes. It can take up to 2 hours for meat to cook. Serve over buttered rice

Parmesan Duck Breast

2		duck breasts, boned and sliced	1		egg beaten with 1 tsp. water
1/4	cup	parmesan cheese	1	cup	oil for frying

Heat oil in heavy skillet. Dip pieces of duck breast in beaten egg and roll in Parmesan cheese. Fry in hot oil.

Quail or Dove Casserole

3	lbs	quail or dove	1	15-oz can	artichokes
1½	tsp	salt	¼	lb	mushrooms
		salt and freshly ground black pepper	2	tbl	flour
½	tsp	paprika	2/3	cup	chicken consomme
6	tbl	butter	3 or 4	tbl	sherry

Salt, pepper, and paprika quail or dove and fry in 4 tbsp. butter. Place in casserole. Place artichokes between quail or dove. Saute mushrooms in 2 tbsp. butter. Add 2 tbsp. flour. Stir in consomme and sherry. Cook 5 minutes. Pour over quail or dove. Cover and cook at 350° for 1 hour.

Rabbit With Dark Raisin Gravy

1 to 2		rabbits cut into quarters	2		bay leaves
1/2	cup	vinegar	1/2	tsp	allspice
2	tsp	salt	1/2	cup	dark raisins
1	tbl	minced onion flakes	1/4	cup	brown sugar
4		whole cloves			

Place rabbit pieces in deep pot and cover with cool water. Add 1/4 cup of vinegar to water and bring to a boil. Let boil 5 minutes. THROW THIS WATER AWAY! Again, cover rabbit with cool water and add 1/4 cup vinegar, 2 tsp. salt, onion, cloves, bay leaves, and allspice. Cook until almost tender and then add raisins and brown sugar. Continue cooking until rabbit is tender and done. Remove rabbit from pot and thicken liquid with a paste of flour and water. Replace rabbit in thickened gravy and heat just before serving.

Roast Pheasant In Orange Gravy

2		pheasants	1	cup	apple, chopped
1	tbl	butter, melted			Orange Gravy:
Apple-Celery Dressing:			2	tbl	cornstarch
4	cups	seasoned stuffing mix	1	cup	orange juice
1/2	cup	onion, chopped	1/4	cup	brown sugar, firmly packed
1		egg, lightly beaten	1	cup	chicken broth
1/2	cup	butter	1/3	cup	orange rind, julienned
1/2	cup	celery, chopped	3	tbl	dry white wine

| 1 | cup | boiling water | | 1/4 | cup | granulated sugar |

Prepare stuffing and spoon lightly into pheasant cavaties. Place birds breast side up on rack in roasting pan and brush with melted butter. Roast covered 2-3 hrs. at 325° or until internal temperature of stuffing reaches 165 °. Lard birds or baste frequently. Serve with orange gravy

To make dressing: toss together stuffing mix and apple in a large bowl. Melt margarine in a small skillet; add celery, and onion and stir frequently 2-3 minutes until tender, then add to stuffing mixture. Stir in water and egg until well blended.

To make gravy: remove pheasants and place on serving platter to keep warm. Drain drippings from roasting pan, leaving brown particles in pan and sprinkle with cornstarch. Stir and cook over medium heat until just blended, then remove from heat. Gradually stir in chicken broth, orange juice, orange rind, sugars, and wine. Return to heat; stirring constantly, bring to a boil. Boil 1 minute.

Smothered Rabbit

1		dressed rabbit cut in pieces		1	med	onion sliced
		seasoned flour		1	cup	sour cream
5	tbl	oil				

Dress and cut 1 rabbit into pieces, dredge with seasoned flour, saute in 3 tablespoons of drippings or butter until brown. Cover thickly with sliced onions, cover with 1 cup sour cream. Cover tightly and simmer for 1 hour in the cream. Cover skillet tightly and simmer for 1 hour or until tender at 300°.

Squirrel Pot Pie

2		dressed squirrels		dash	black pepper
2 1/2	cups	water			rolled dumplings
1 1/2	tsp	salt			parsley
2	tbl	butter			

Great way to cook older squirrels that are too tough for frying. Wipe thoroughly with a damp cloth and remove all hair. Remove any shot and scent glands. Wash well inside and out with warm water. Cut into serving pieces. Put squirrel into a kettle; add water and salt; heat to boiling. Reduce heat; cover tightly and simmer until very tender (2-3 hours depending on age of animal). The meat should be almost ready to fall from the bones.

Add pepper and butter. Increase the heat until liquid boils. Lay the rolled dumplings over the top of squirrel; cover tightly and cook for 12-15 minutes. Do not lift cover during cooking. Place squirrel in a hot plate and arrange dumplings around the edge. Cooking the dumplings in the liquid should thicken the gravy to just the right consistency. Pour gravy over squirrel and dumplings. A little fresh chopped parsley may be sprinkled over the top for garnish.

Squirrel With Rice And Potatoes

| 2 | | squirrels, cut up | | 1 | cup | uncooked rice |
| | | fat | | 1 | | green pepper chopped |

1		onion chopped		3	med	potatoes chopped
1		green pepper chopped				salt and pepper
1/4	cup	chopped celery				water
1	clove	garlic chopped				

Brown squirrels in skillet with small amount of fat. Place squirrel in pressure cooker and cook under pressure for 15 minutes to tenderize. Saute onion, green pepper, celery, and garlic in drippings in skillet; add rice, squirrel, potatoes, seasonings, and enough liquid to cook rice and potatoes. Cover; simmer slowly until tender.

Venison Chili

2	med	onions, chopped, sautéd		1 1/2	tsp	paprika
		salt and pepper to taste			dash	Lea & Perrins
2	med	green peppers, chopped, sautéd		4	cans	tomatoes diced
3	tsp	garlic powder		1	can	tomato paste
3	lbs	ground venison browned		1	bottle	ketchup
1/2	tsp	oregano		1	lg can	pinto beans
1	tsp	ground red pepper		1	lg can	red kidney beans
5	tsp	chili powder				

Mix all ingredients and add as much of your favorite liquid hot sauce as you and your doctor see fit. Cover; simmer over low heat 3 hrs. Best refrigerated 1+ days after cooking and reheated prior to serving. Scrve with grated cheese and/or chopped onions.

Venison Meat Balls

1	lb	ground venison		2	tbl	soy sauce
1	cup	bread crumbs				garlic powder to taste
1/2	tsp	salt		1/4	cup	butter
1/4	tsp	pepper		1	tbl	flour
2/3	cup	onion, finely chopped		1	cup	milk

Combine crumbs, venison, salt, pepper, onion, soy sauce, and garlic powder; shape into balls about 1" in diameter. Brown meatballs in butter, cover pan; cook over low heat 15 minutes. Remove meatballs from pan and add flour to drippings to make gravy. Add milk and simmer 3-4 minutes (without boiling). Serve gravy hot over the meat balls. Try adding allspice, ginger, nutmeg, cloves, brown sugar, oregano, and other spices for variety.

Venison, Elk or Moose Roast

3	lb	roast		1/2	pkg dry onion soup

Preheat oven to 425. Place roast on piece of heavy duty aluminum foil. Sprinkle 1/2 pkg of dry onion soup over meat. Bring edges of foil together and seal tightly. Place in shallow roasting pan and bake for 2 to 2 1/2 hours. There will be ample juice collected inside foil which can be thickened for gravy.

Wild Duck with Gin Marmalade

2		wild ducks	2		apples
2	quarts	water	1	cup	gin
1	tbl	salt	2	12 oz jars	orange marmalade
2		onions			

Put ducks, water and salt in a 4-quart kettle. Bring to a boil and boil for 5 to 7 minutes. Remove ducks and stuff with onion and apple. Place ducks in roaster, breast up. Pour gin over ducks and coat each duck liberally with marmalade. Cover and roast in slow oven at 325° for 2 hours or until tender.

Miscellaneous

Blue Cheese or Roquefort Dressing

1/4	lb	Roquefort or Blue cheese	2	cups	sour cream
1		small onion, grated	1/2	cup	mayonnaise
		Juice of 2 lemons			salt and pepper

Mix all ingredients in blender. Will keep refrigerated for 1 month.

(Note, if you like chunky dressing...mix 1/2 of the cheese with the remaining ingredients in blender, then add the remainder of the crumbled cheese at the end.)

Buttermilk Garlic Salad Dressing

1/2	cup	sour cream	1	tbl	sugar
1/2	cup	mayonnaise	1/2	tsp	dry mustard powder
1	cup	low-fat buttermilk	1/4	tsp	paprika
1	clove	garlic			kosher salt and pepper to taste

Combine in a blender. Will keep for a week or more.

Chicken Gruel

1½	cup	plain cornmeal		chicken stock
4 to 5		chicken thighs		salt and black pepper to taste

Boil chicken. Cool and remove chicken from bones and shred (or chop) into small pieces. Add cornmeal, salt and pepper to stock (about 3 cups) and whisk until no lumps are seen. Bring to a boil and add chicken. Lower heat to medium and cook until thick and creamy. Whisk constantly to avoid sticking.

Cucumber Chow Chow

1		hot pepper	6	stalks	celery finely chopped
5	med	onions	1	tbl	celery seed
1	doz	cucumbers	1	tbl	yellow mustard seed
		salt			vinegar

Finely chop pepper, onions and cucumbers. Salt and let stand over night. Drain and add ½ dozen stalks of celery. Add celery seed and yellow mustard seed. Cover with vinegar and cook over low heat, but do not bring to a boil.

Pour mixture into jars and seal.

No specific amounts were given for some ingredients. This was a "dump and taste" recipe

Egg Gravy

Verna Albritton Hickox

| 1 or 2 | eggs | water to thicken |
| | flour | salt and pepper to taste |

Scramble eggs in oil. Push to one side of pan. In the other side brown flour in a little oil. Add water to eggs and flour mixture to thicken stirring all the time. Season to taste with salt and pepper.

Great over hot biscuits

Fried Cornmeal Mush

1 1/4	cup	yellow cornmeal			oil for frying
1	cup	cold water	1/4	cup	all-purpose flour
3	cup	hot water			flour for dredging
1	tsp	salt			

In a small bowl, combine the cornmeal, salt, and ¼ cup flour. Gradually whisk the cold water into the mixture. Bring the hot water to a boil in a large saucepan over high heat and gradually whisk in the cornmeal mixture. Stir and whisk until it boils. Cover, lower heat, and simmer for 5 minutes. The mixture will be very thick. Pour into an oiled 9 x 5 x 3 inch loaf pan and refrigerate overnight.

The next day, cut the loaf into 1/2 inch slices. In a skillet, heat 2 tsp of oil or bacon fat. Dredge 3 or 4 slices in the flour and fry them over low heat until golden brown on both sides. Continue to cook remaining mush, adding oil to the skillet as needed. Serve with either maple syrup or Tomato Gravy.

Giblet Gravy

	giblets from chicken or hen	1	cup	drippings
3 tbl	butter	1	cup	chicken broth
3 tbl	flour			salt and black pepper to taste

Put giblets in saucepan and add water to cover. Salt slightly. Simmer for 30 minutes or until tender. Melt the butter in a large saucepan then sprinkle in the flour. Stir until flour is a light brown. Add drippings and chicken stock. Cook over medium heat, stirring constantly, until the gravy is smooth and thickened. Reduce heat and add giblets. Add salt and pepper and simmer for 10 minutes

Grits

1 cup grits 3 cups water 1 cup ah milk 1 teaspoons salt 1 tablespoon butter First you needs ta go get a bag ah grits from the local griss mill. This is the real thang and not that there instant stuff. Maw says ya get your water ta boilin on a medium boil first. When it is den ya pore in ya cup ah grits in real slow. Maw says ta make sure ya never stop stirrin now. To make your grits nice and creamy jess add a few spirts from the cows tits. You can use dat there can stuff if ya wants to but the best cream will be the better.

Now we knows the instructions on grits will tell ya to boil ferr a certain amount of time but Maw says to tell ya that what ever them directions say..... ta make sure ya double that boilin time. Now if your boilin is goin to fast denn it will be spittin out grits like firein rat shot at foxes in the hen house! And talk bout hurtin! Why them grits will stick to ya like white on rice so it's best ya make sure ya got your boilin temp jess right. Now, put your salt in and your butter in and surve it up while its hot. If you lets it get cold it will soon look like jelled jello and youins don't want dat.

Source

Author: Hillbilly Recipe' Collection
Web Page: http://www.gone-ta-pott.com/hillbillyrecipes.html
Copyright: © written by: P. R. P. Svoboda

Homemade Ranch Dressing

1/2	tsp	pepper	2	tbl	water
1/2	tsp	dill weed	2/3	cup	buttermilk
1/2	tsp	dried parsley	1/3	cup	mayonnaise
1/2	tsp	dried basil	1	tbl	cider vinegar
1/2	tsp	thyme	1	tsp	Dijon mustard
1/4	tsp	minced garlic	1	tsp	sugar
1/4	tsp	paprika	1/4	tsp	salt

Put water in a small bowl and add spices and herbs. Whisk and allow to set for 5 minutes. Pour buttermilk and mayonnaise into a bowl and whisk well. Add water/herb/spice mixture, vinegar, mustard, sugar and salt. Whisk well until smooth. Pout into a jar and shake well. Store in refrigerator for one week.

Ketchup

1	can	tomato paste	¼	tsp	dry mustard
¼	cup	water	¼	tsp	cinnamon
¼	cup	brown sugar	1/8	tsp	cloves
½	tsp	salt	2	tbl	cider vinegar
¼	tsp	cumin			

Mix all ingredients together and stir until brown sugar dissolves. Pour into bottle and refrigerate

Maple Syrup

1	cup	brown sugar firmly packed	¼	tsp	maple flavoring
½	tsp	water			

Combine sugar and water in saucepan. Bring to a boil. Stir until sugar dissolves. Remove from heat. Stir in flavoring.

Mayonnaise

2	egg yolks	pinch	cayenne pepper

¾	tsp	salt	4 to 5	tsp	vinegar or lemon juice
¼	tsp	mustard powder	1½	cups	oil, divided
1/8	tsp	sugar	4	tbl	hot water

Beat yolks, salt, mustard, sugar, pepper, and 1 teaspoon lemon juice in a small bowl until very thick and pale yellow. (Note: If using electric mixer, beat at medium speed.) Add about ¼ cup oil, drop by drop, beating vigorously all the while. Beat in 1 teaspoon each lemon juice and hot water. Add another ¼ cup oil, a few drops at a time, beating vigorously all the while. Beat in another teaspoon each lemon juice and water. Add ½ cup oil in a very fine steady stream, beating constantly, then mix in remaining lemon juice and water; slowly beat in remaining oil. If you like, thin mayonnaise with a little additional hot water. Cover and refrigerate until needed. Do not keep longer than 1 week.

Pear Butter

1	gallon	pears peeled and quartered	cinnamon
4	gallons	water	cloves
5	lbs	sugar	nutmeg

Peel and quarter pears and place in 4 gallons of water with 5 pounds of sugar. Bring mixture to a boil and continue cooking over low heat until the liquid gradually thickens. (cloves, cinnamon and nutmeg is often added for spicy flavoring)

When the mixture is thick, pour into quart jars and seal.

Pot Likker

liquid from cooked collards or turnips   onion chopped
cornbread crumbled

Separate liquid from cooked collard greens or turnip greens. Heat. Crumble cornbread into liquid and eat as a soup. You may also add chopped onions for extra zing. Serve with fried pork chop, country smoked ham and baked sweet potato

Red Eye Gravy

Add black coffee to fried ham drippings in a hot pan. Let sizzle and stir. Serve with country cured fried ham slices, and biscuits.

Salad Dressing

¾	cup	oil	1	tsp	salt
½	cup	vinegar	½	cup	ketchup
½	cup	sugar	1	tsp	celery seed
1	tbl	onion minced	¼	cup	water
1		garlic clove, minced		dash	Worcestershire sauce
½	tsp	mustard			

Mix together. Shake in a covered jar or whirl in blender for a few seconds. Refrigerate

Sausage Gravy

1	lb	bulk pork sausage	1	cup	milk
1	tbl	flour			salt and black pepper to taste

Brown sausage. Remove sausage from pan. Drain off all but 2 to 3 tbs drippings. Add flour to drippings and brown for about 1 minute. Add salt and pepper to taste. Slowly pour in milk stirring constantly until thick. Add sausage and mix well. Serve over hot split biscuits

Spicy Tartar Sauce

1	cup	mayonnaise	2	tbs	horseradish
4	tbs	sweet relish			

Mix together and serve with seafood. Great with seafood or french fries

Tomato Gravy

1	can	tomatoes diced	salt and black pepper to taste
3	tbs	flour	

Brown flour in bacon drippings. Add salt and pepper. Add water to browned flour and stir until thick. Add tomatoes and simmer for a few minutes. Serve over hot biscuits

Tomato Gruel

1½	cups	plain cornmeal			salt and black pepper to taste
		hot water	1	can	crushed tomatoes

Mix cornmeal with just enough water to make moist. Put into large boiler. Add 3 cups boiling water. Bring to a boil whisking to avoid sticking. Add tomatoes, salt and pepper. Cook on medium heat until thick and creamy

Zero Salad Dressing

½	cup	tomato juice	½	cup	bell pepper, seeded and finely chopped
2	tbl	lemon juice or vinegar	1	tbl	parsley minced
1	tbl	onion finely chopped	1	tbl	horseradish
	dash	black pepper			garlic to taste if desired

Mix all ingredients and shake well in jar. Refrigerate

Soups & Salads

Apple Lettuce Salad

½	cup	unsweetened apple juice	¼	tsp	cinnamon
2	tbl	lemon juice		dash	nutmeg
2	tbl	apple cider vinegar	1	med	red apple, chopped
2	tbl	canola oil	1	med	green apple chopped
5	tsp	brown sugar	6	cups	green leaf lettuce torn
1	tsp	Dijon mustard	6	cups	red leaf lettuce torn
¼	tsp	salt			

In a large salad bowl, whisk the first 10 ingredients until blended. Add apples; toss to coat. Place lettuce over apple mixture (do not toss). Refrigerate; toss just before serving

Brunswick Stew

1	sm	pork roast	1	can	carrots
1	sm	beef roast	6	lg	potatoes cut in large pieces
4		chicken breasts -- boned and skinned	2	cans	tomatoes diced
1	lg	onion chopped	½	sm	bottle ketchup
1	can	butterbeans			salt and black pepper to taste
1	can	english peas	¼	bottle	hot sauce
2	cans	shoepeg corn	¼	bottle	Worcestershire sauce

Cook all meats until about "half done" and cut into pieces. Put back in liquid. Add remaining ingredients to the meat in a large stew pot. Add liquid as needed. Cook over low heat stirring often. Meat will shred while cooking. Add more hot sauce if desired

Butter Soup

8	cups	water			Parsley chopped
1	lg	onion	**Noodles**		
6	med	potatoes skin left on	1	lg	egg
1	lg	bay leaf	2	tbl	water
5		whole cloves	1	cup	flour
8		peppercorns	1/2	tsp	salt
1		star aniseed			

Bring water to boil, add the onion and diced potatoes. Simmer 15 minutes. Add all the spices but the parsley, wrapped and tied in cheesecloth. Let simmer while you make the noodles. Add the chopped parsley to the soup separately from the cheesecloth.

Stir together the egg water, salt and stir in half the flour and then dump it onto the counter and knead in the rest of the flour. You may need a little more.

Cut it strips with clean scissors, some small and others bigger. Stir the noodles into the soup, bring to boil and boil a few minutes until the noodles are done. Ladle it into bowls, and put a dollop of butter onto the top, serve with a bit of fresh cream.

Buttermilk Salad

1	lg box	Jello any flavor	2	cups	buttermilk
1	sm can	crushed pineapple, do not drain	1	lg	frozen whipped topping

Mix dry jello (do not add water) and crushed pineapple (do not drain) and bring to a boil. Let cool. Mix buttermilk with whipped topping. Add to cooled jello mixture. Pour into lightly greased mold or casserole dish. Chill

Crawfish and Corn Chowder

1	lb	crawfish tails, peeled or seafood of choice	2	pints	half-and-half or light cream
	12 oz	bacon, fried and crumbled	2	tbl	butter
2	cups	potatoes peeled and cut into 1/2-inch cubes			Creole seasoning to taste
1	lg	sweet onion chopped			milk as needed to thin chowder
2	cans	shoepeg corn			

Fry bacon until crisp. Discard all but 4 tbsp of bacon grease. Sauté' potatoes and onions until almost tender. Add butter, corn, Half & Half and seasonings. Crumble bacon into fine bits and add to chowder. Cook until potatoes are tender; approximately 20-30 minutes. Add crawfish and continue to cook 15-20 minutes before serving (best not to overcook crawfish.) For an added delight, serve chowder in bread bowls.

Fruit Medley

1 8-oz can	fruit cocktail, drained	1	cup	miniature marshmallows
1 4 oz container	frozen whipped topping	¼	cup	milk
1 cup	coconut			

Combine all ingredients (mix well). Chill about 1 hour

Garden Chickpea Salad

6	cups	spring salad mix	**tomato vinaigrette**		
1½	cups	chickpeas or garbonzo beans drained	½	cup	lemon juice
1	cup	parsley sprigs chopped	½	cup	olive oil
2	med	carrots, julienned	2		garlic clove, minced
2	sm	zuchini julienned	½	tsp	cumin
4		green onions (scallions), sliced	1	tsp	salt
			½	tsp	red pepper

½	cup	feta cheese, crumbled
½	cup	radishes thinly sliced
6	tbl	walnuts, roughly chopped

Divide greens between four salad plates. Combine the chickpeas, parsley, carrot, zucchini, onions, cheese, radishes and walnuts. In a small bowl, combine the vinaigrette ingredients. Pour half over chickpea mixture and toss to coat. Spoon chickpea mixture over greens. Drizzle salads with remaining vinaigrette. Serve immediately.

Hamburger Soup with Black-Eyed Peas and Kale

1	lb	ground beef		1	can	tomatoes diced
1	med	onion chopped		1	can	black eyed peas, drained
2	med	carrots peeled and diced		1	cup	whole kernel corn
2	cups	kale chopped				Salt and black pepper to taste
2	cups	beef broth				

Heat oil in a large saucepan or Dutch oven over medium-low heat. Add beef and onion; saute, stirring, until the ground beef is browned. Add garlic and carrots and cook for 1 minute longer. Add the beef broth and bring to a boil. Simmer for 10 minutes. Add the kale, tomatoes, peas, corn, and seasonings. Cover and simmer for 20 to 25 minutes.

Low Country Boil

4	lbs	small red potatoes		1	doz	ears mini sweet corn
5	quarts	water		4	lbs	shrimp (21 to 25), peeled and deveined
1	bag	Crab Boil seasoning or Creole seasoning to taste				Cocktail sauce
4	tbl	Old Bay seasoning				
2	lbs	Kielbasa sausage, sliced on diagonal or hot smoked link sausage				

Add potatoes to large pot, then add 5 quarts water and seasonings. Cover pot and heat to a rolling boil; cook 5 minutes. Add sausage and corn, and return to a boil. Cook 10 minutes or until potatoes are tender. Add shrimp to stockpot; cook 3 to 4 minutes or until shrimp turn pink. Drain. Serve with cocktail sauce

Old Fashioned Vegetable Soup

This soup can be made with left-over, fresh or canned vegetables

butterbeans	celery chopped
peas	tomatoes diced
green beans	potatoes peeled and cut into 1/2-inch cubes
corn	Salt and black pepper to taste
okra	

Combine ingredients in one quart of water, salt and pepper to taste. When using fresh vegetables cook until potatoes are soft. For canned and left over vegetables, heat for ten minutes Serve with cornbread

Reception Salad

3	sm pkgs	lime jello	1	sm jar	chopped pimento drained
1	cup	celery finely chopped		12 oz	cheddar cheese, grated
2	lg cans	crushed pineapple	1	pint	whipping cream
1 1/3	cups	nuts, finely chopped			

Drain juice from pineaple and bring to a boil. Add 1 cup hot water. Pour over jello to dissolve. Stir and place in refrigerator until it begins to gel. Whip the cream while jello is cooling. Once jello has begun to gel add remaining ingredients and mix well. Pour into greased mold or casserole dish

Rick's Fruit Salad

Mix a variety of canned fruits (drain) in a large bowl. Add chopped nuts, mini marshmallows and coconut. Stir and chill. Great as a side to pound cake

Taco Soup

2	lbs	ground beef	1	can	tomatoes diced
1	lg	sweet onion chopped	1	can	Rotel tomatoes
1	can	pinto beans	1	pkg	taco seasoning mix
1	can	black beans	1	pkg	Hidden Valley Original Ranch dressing dry
1	can	kidney beans			
1	can	shoepeg corn	2½	cups	water

Brown ground beef and onions in a large pan, drain off fat. Add remaining ingredients and simmer for an hour or so. When ready, serve in big soup bowls. Great with a dollop of sour cream. Add cornbread and you have the perfect cold weather meal

Freezes well

Tomato Bacon Soup

6	slices	bacon	1	can	chicken broth
½	cup	sweet onion chopped	¼	tsp	sugar
2	tbl	flour			salt and black pepper to taste
1	lg can	crushed tomatoes			

Fry bacon and drain. Chop into pieces. Saute onions and flour in bacon drippings. Add remaining ingredients and simmer for 15 to 20 minutes. Sprinkle bacon on top of soup.

Vegetables & Side Dishes

Asparagus Casserole

1	cup	asparagus spears, drained		**White Sauce**		
1	tsp	pimento, chopped		2	tbl	butter
2	cups	cheddar cheese grated		2	tbl	flour
2	cups	white sauce		1¼	cups	milk, heated
2		eggs, boiled and sliced				salt and black pepper to taste
		cracker crumbs				

Place the asparagus in a greased casserole. Add half the pimiento and one egg. Sprinkle half the cheese and cover with 1 cup white sauce. Make second layer same as first. Sprinkle with cracker crumbs. Bake at 350 for 20 minutes

To make White Sauce: Melt the butter in a heavy-bottomed saucepan. Stir in the flour and cook, stirring constantly, until the paste cooks and bubbles a bit, but don't let it brown — about 2 minutes. Add the hot milk, continuing to stir as the sauce thickens. Bring it to a boil. Add salt and pepper to taste, lower the heat, and cook, stirring for 2 to 3 minutes more. Remove from the heat.

Baked Cabbage

1	lb	coarsely shredded cabbage		1 ¼ cups	milk	
1	tsp	salt		1	tsp	prepared mustard
2	tbl	butter		½	cup	cheddar cheese grated
2	tbl	flour dash of pepper		2	tbl	fine corn flake crumbs

Cook cabbage in small amount of boiling water for 8 to 10 minutes or just until tender. Drain. Sprinkle with ½ tsp salt.Melt butter and stir in flour, remaining ½ tsp salt and pepper. Add milk and mustard and cook until thickened,stirring constantly. Combine cabbage, sauce and half the cheese. Spoon into buttered round 1-quart casserole

Sprinkle with remaining cheese mixed with crumbs. Bake at 350° for 20 to 25 minutes or until hot and bubbly

Baked Pineapple

2	21 oz can	pineapple chunks, drained		2	cups	Ritz Crackers coarsely broken
½	cup	flour		1	stick	butter
½	cup	sugar		1	sm block	cream cheese, softened
2	cups	cheddar cheese, grated				

Put pineapple in baking dish. Mix flour, sugar, cream cheese and cheese. Sprinkle over pineapple. Mix crackers and margarine and sprinkle over top. Bake at 325° for about 30 minutes or until hot and bubbly.

Birdie's Baked Beans

Birdie Lisenby Earnest

1	lg can	pork n beans	1/3	cup	light brown sugar
1	8-oz can	tomato sauce	8 to 10	slices	bacon cut in 2" pieces
1		onion chopped			

Spray baking dish with Pam and preheat oven to 425 °. Mix all ingredients and put in dish. Top with bacon and bake.

Brown Rice

1	stick	butter	1	cake	beef consomme
1	cup	onion chopped	1	can	water
1	cup	rice	1	can	mushrooms sliced

Melt butter. Add onions and cook on low until onion is clear. Add rice, stirring well. Take off heat. Add consommé and water. Add mushrooms. Mix well. Pour into casserole dish and bake at 350° for 45 minutes or until rice is tender

Butter Bean Casserole

2	slices	bacon cut in 2" pieces	1	can	tomatoes diced
1	med	sweet onion chopped	½	tsp	salt
½		bell pepper, chopped	2	tsp	sugar
1	bag	frozen butter beans		dash	pepper

Saute bacon, onion and bell pepper until tender and bacon is brown. Pour beans and tomatoes into baking dish. Add salt, sugar, pepper and bacon. Mix and bake at 300° for 40 minutes or until beans are tender

Butternut Squash

1½	lbs	butternut squash peeled and cut into 1-inch cubes	½	tsp	salt
2	tbl	all purpose flour	½	cup	bread crumbs
2	tbl	lemon juice	2	tbl	broth
1	tsp	cinnamon	½	tsp	nutmeg

Heat oven to 350°. Spray square pan, 8x8x2 inches, with nonstick cooking spray. Mix all ingredients except bread crumbs and broth; spread in pan. Bake uncovered about 50 minutes or until squash is tender. Mix bread crumbs and broth; spread over squash. Set oven control to broil. Broil squash with tops about 4 inches from heat about 3 minutes or until bread crumbs are brown. Serve in covered dish to keep warm.

Cabbage Rolls

1	lg	cabbage	1 1/2	tsp	salt	
2	lbs	lean ground beef	1	tsp	pepper	
2	med	onions	2	cans	tomato soup	
2	tbl	oil	2	sm bottles	tomato juice or V8	
1	cup	cooked rice	1	can	chicken broth	
3		eggs				

Place cabbage in a bag and freeze for 12 hours or overnight. Remove and leave to thaw at room temperature. The leaves will be soft and easy to use without having to boil them.

Cook rice and set aside. Chop the onions fine and saute them slowly until they are golden brown.

In a large bowl, break apart the ground beef, add the salt, pepper, eggs, sauteed onions and the rice. Mix together until combined.

Remove the leaves from the cabbage, cutting away the tough part closest to the core. Spray your large casserole or two small casserole dishes with cooking spray. Put about a 1/3 to 1/2 cup meat mixture at the bottom of the leaf and roll up. Repeat until all the meat is used up.

In a large mixing bowl combine the tomato soup, juice, and broth. Pour evenly over the cabbage rolls. Cover with foil. Bake the cabbage rolls slowly at 325° for two hours.

Collards

2	bunches	fresh collards	¾	cup	oil
		smoked neckbone or ham hock	1	tbl	sugar optional
		salt to taste			

Cut hard vein from collards. Wash leaves in several sinks of water until all grit is gone. If you can feel any grit in the bottom of the sink they are clean. Usually takes 4 to 6 sinks depending on how dirty they are. Put in large pot and add salt and neckbone and oil. Cover with water and bring to a boil. Reduce to a slow boil and add sugar. Boil until tender.

Corn and Tomato Bake

2	cups	cooked whole corn	1	tsp	sugar
2	cups	chopped tomatoes	1	cup	fresh bread crumbs
1	tsp	salt	2	tbl	butter
		pepper			

Combine corn and tomatoes with salt, pepper, and sugar; pour all into a greased baking dish. Sprinkle the bread crumbs over mixture and dot with the butter. Bake in a 350° oven for 30 minutes.

Corn Casserole

3		eggs beaten	1	can	whole kernel corn
¼	cup	flour	1	can	creamed corn

| 2 | tsp | sugar | 1 | tbl | butter |
| 1½ | cups | cheddar cheese grated | | | salt and black pepper to taste |

Preheat oven to 350°. Lightly grease casserole dish. Mix all ingredients (reserving some of the cheese) and pour into dish. Top with cheese. Bake until set

Corn Fritters

1 1/3	cups	buttermilk baking mix	1		egg, beaten
1 1/2	tsp	baking powder	1	cup	vegetable oil
1	can	cream-style corn	1 1/2	cups	maple syrup

In a medium mixing bowl, sift together baking mix and baking powder. In a small mixing bowl, combine corn and egg. Combine egg and flour mixture, stir gently. Heat oil in large skillet over medium heat. Drop batter by tablespoonfuls into hot oil one layer at a time. Fry for 2 minutes on each side or until golden brown. Drain fritters on absorbent paper. Serve immediately with maple syrup or molasses.

Cornbread Dressing

1	batch	eggbread	1	tbl	poultry seasoning
1		onion chopped	1	tsp	sage
2	stalks	celery chopped	2		boiled eggs chopped
3 to 4	cups	chicken broth	1	can	cream of chicken soup, no water added
		salt and black pepper to taste			

Make a batch of eggbread. While the bread is cooking, chop onions, celery and eggs. When cornbread is brown remove from oven and cut into large pieces and place in mixing bowl. Crumble bread and add chopped ingredients and seasonings. Add chicken broth and stir. Add more seasonings as needed.   For extra creaminess add 1 can cream of chicken soup. Mix well. Pour into lightly oiled baking dish. Bake at 350° until golden brown

Creamed Onions

6	med	onions, sliced	½	tsp	salt
¼	cup	butter	¼	tsp	pepper
3	tbl	flour self rising	1	cup	cheddar cheese shredded
1 ½	cups	milk			

Saute' onion in butter in a sauce pan over until tender. Reduce heat, sprinkle flour over onion and stir until smooth. Cook 1 minute, stirring constantly. Gradually add milk, stirring until smooth. Stir in salt and pepper. Cook, stirring constantly, until thickened. Stir in cheese until melted, if desired.

Serve with meatloaf, hamburger steaks and biscuits or grits.

Creamy Coleslaw

1/2	cup	mayonnaise or salad dressing	1/4	tsp	salt	
1/4	cup	sour cream	1/4	tsp	pepper	
1	tbl	sugar	4	cups	cabbage, finely shredded or chopped	
2	tsp	lemon juice	1	sm	carrot, shredded	
2	tsp	Dijon mustard	1	sm	onion, chopped	
1/2	tsp	celery seed				

Mix all ingredients except cabbage, carrot and onion in large glass or plastic bowl. Add remaining ingredients; toss until evenly coated. Cover and refrigerate at least 1 hour to blend flavors. Cover and refrigerate any remaining salad.

Easy Bean Salad

1	can	french style green beans, drained	1	cup	celery finely chopped
1	can	Chinese vegetables, drained	½	cup	vinegar
1	can	english peas, drained	½	cup	sugar
1	cup	onion chopped			salt and black pepper to taste

Drain vegetables and put in bowl. Add onions and celery. Mix vinegar and sugar and pour over vegetables. Marinate in refrigerator overnight.

Eggplant Casserole

2	cups	eggplant, peeled, and cut in 1/2" cubes	1	tbl	onion chopped
6	tbl	butter	1	tsp	salt
1	tsp	pepper	1	cup	cracker crumbs
4	ounces	cheddar cheese cubed	2		eggs beaten
1	cup	milk			

Cook eggplant and drain, add butter while hot, then add all other ingredients. Put in greased casserole and bake at 325° till center rises some. About 45 min

English Pea Casserole

1	can	english peas, drained	8-oz		cheddar cheese grated
3		eggs boiled and sliced	1	can	cream of chicken soup
1	sm jar	pimento, chopped and drained			bread crumbs

In bottom of greased, 1 quart casserole dish, put half of peas, half of the eggs, half the cheese half the pimento. Repeat, using all of these. Dilute the soup according to directions for making sauce. Pour this over the layers in the dish. Sprinkle the bread crumbs over the top and bake at 350° for 20 minutes or until bubbly.

Fried Collard Greens

A Taste From Yesteryear

1	bell pepper, seeded and sliced		4 cups	cooked collard greens
1	onion chopped			

Save drippings from fried bacon or country smoked ham. Place pepper and onion in hot drippings and cook until tender. Pour pepper, onions and drippings over collards in skillet and cook until hot stirring constantly. (about 5 minutes) Serve with a slice of country smoked ham, baked sweet potato and cornbread.

Fried Green Tomatoes

2	green tomatos, sliced thin		1 cup	self rising flour
	Salt and black pepper to taste		1 cup	milk
1 cup	white cornmeal			shortening (for frying tomatoes)

Pat dry tomato slices with paper towel then sprinkle with salt and pepper. Mix flour, meal and milk together to make batter. Add more milk if needed to make pancake consistency. Heat shortening in cast iron skillet. Dip tomato slices into batter and drain off excess and lay in fryer. Brown on both sides and drain on paper towels. Repeat process until all are fried.

Fried Onion Rings

2	cups	self-rising flour		1	egg beaten
2/3	cup	cornmeal		6 lg	onions, peeled and sliced into ¼-inch
½	tsp	salt			slices and separated into rings
½	tsp	pepper			vegetable oil
1 ¾	cups	milk			

Combine first 4 ingredients in a large bowl; beat in milk and egg. Let stand 5 minutes and add onion to batter and toss until onion is well coated. When you are ready to fry them, pick up onion rings and let excess batter drip back into bowl. Place slices immediately in hot oil at 375 ° and deep fry until browned, turning only once. Drain in a colander and sprinkle with additional salt, if desired.

Zucchini may be used in place of onions. Just cut into 1/2–inch slices and prepare same a onoins.

Green Bean Casserole

1 can	cream of mushroom soup, no water added		1 can	onion rings
				salt and black pepper to taste
2 cans	green beans			

Pour soup into a quart casserole. Add 1/2 can onion rings, both cans green beans, & pepper. Mix well. Bake at 350° for 20 minutes. Put the other 1/2 can onion rings on top and bake 5 minutes longer.

Green Chile Casserole

6	cups	boiling water		1	stick	butter
2	tsp	salt		1½	cups	grits
1	lb	Velveeta		3		eggs beaten
1	can	green chilies diced				

Bring water to a boil, add grits and cook slowly until thick. Add cheese (cut in pieces), green chilies and oleo, stir until cheese melts. Beat in eggs. Pour into buttered casserole and bake 1 hour at 275°

Green Rice

1	cup	onion chopped		2	cups	rice cooked
1	cup	celery finely chopped		1	can	Rotel tomatoes
1	stick	butter				black and red pepper to taste
1	bag	frozen broccoli				salt to taste
2	cans	cream of chicken soup		1	cup	cheddar cheese, grated
1	8-oz jar	Cheez Whiz				

Saute celery and onion in butter. Cook broccoli according to package directions and drain. Add soup and cheese whiz to celery and onions. Add broccoli, tomatoes and cooked rice. Add salt, black and red pepper to taste. Heat in moderate oven to melt cheese

Hoppin John

2	cups	dried black eye peas		2		smoked ham hocks
10	cups	water		1	lg	onion chopped
1	tsp	red pepper		2	cups	rice

Wash and sort the peas. Place them in the saucepan, add the water, and discard any peas that float. Gently boil the peas with the pepper, ham hock, and onion, uncovered, until tender but not mushy — about 1½ hours — or until 2 cups of liquid remain. Add the rice to the pot, cover, and simmer over low heat for about 20 minutes, never lifting the lid. Remove from the heat and allow to steam, still covered, for another 10 minutes. Remove the cover, fluff with a fork, and serve immediately.

Macaroni and Cheese

1	8 oz box	macaroni, cooked according to directions, drained		¾	cup	sharp cheddar cheese grated
3	tbl	butter		¾	cup	pepper jack cheese, grated
1	tsp	salt			dash	red pepper
1		egg		½	cup	milk

Boil macaroni in salted water until desired tenderness. Drain in cold water to avoid sticking. Mix remaining ingredients with macaroni. Pour into greased baking dish. Top with buttered bread crumbs. Bake at 350° until brown

Pepper Cabbage

1	sm	head cabbage, chopped	1	tbl	vinegar
2		green peppers chopped			salt and black pepper to taste
4	stalks	celery chopped			

Chop a head of cabbage, 2 green peppers, and several stalks of celery. Add 1 Tbsp of vinegar and cook until the vegetables are tender. Add salt and pepper to taste. Seal in jars while hot

Pineapple Casserole

1	cup	butter	1½	cups	sugar
1	lg can	crushed pineapple drained thoroughly	4	cups	soft bread crumbs
3		eggs	¼	pint	half-and-half or light cream

Cream butter and sugar. Add eggs, one at a time, beating after each addition. Mix in drained pineapple, bread crumbs and half and half. Bake in lightly greased dish at 350° for 1 hour

Potato Salad

5	lbs	potatoes, peeled and chopped	1	sm jar	sweet pickles, drained and chopped
10		eggs	2	cups	mayonnaise
½	cup	celery chopped fine	1	sm jar	pimento drained

Place the potatoes in a large pan of water and boil over medium-low heat until tender, about 12 minutes. Drain the potatoes, and place in the refrigerator to cool.

Place the eggs in a saucepan of salted cold water over medium heat, and bring to a full boil. Turn off the heat, cover the pan, and allow the eggs to sit in the hot water for about 15 minutes. Cool the eggs thoroughly under cold running water and shell them. Chop the cooled eggs and place them in a large salad bowl.

Stir the sweet pickles, pimento, and mayonnaise into the eggs, and let the mixture chill in the refrigerator at least 1/2 hour to blend the flavors. Mix in the chilled chopped potatoes, and refrigerate for at least 1/2 hour. Serve cold.

Scalloped Potatoes

1	can	cream of celery soup	1		onion thinly sliced
½	cup	milk	1	cup	cheddar cheese, grated
4	cups	potatos thinly sliced			salt and black pepper to taste

Blend soup, milk, salt and pepper. Arrange alternate layers of potatoes. Onions, Soup mixture and cheese in a buttered casserole dish. Bake at 375° about 45 minutes. Uncover and bake about 15 minutes more

Scalloped Squash

4	cups	cooked squash diced			salt and pepper to taste
2	tbl	onion	½	cup	cheese grated
½		stick margarine	2	cups	white sauce

Cook onion in margarine until transparent, but not brown. Mix with squash, salt and pepper. Put in buttered casserole and cover with sauce then cheese. Top with buttered bread or cracker crumbs. Bake at 375 until it is bubbling and brown.

Skunk Cabbage

1	sm	head cabbage, chopped			salt and black pepper to taste
1	med	onion chopped	6 to 8	slices	bacon fried and crumbled
4 to 5	tbl	bacon grease			

Fry bacon and crumble. Pour off all grease but 4 to 5 tbl. Add chopped cabbage and chopped onion to pan. Salt and pepper to taste. Stir fry until nearly soft. Add additional bacon grease if needed to keep from sticking. Add crumbled bacon and toss. Remove from heat. Do not over cook cabbage

Smothered Cabbage

1	med	head cabbage, cut into wedges			black pepper freshly ground, to taste
½	cup	bell pepper, chopped	2	cups	milk
½	cup	onion chopped	½	cup	mayonnaise
4	tbl	butter	½	cup	cheddar cheese, grated
¼	cup	flour	¼	cup	chili sauce
½	tsp	salt			

Cook cabbage in salted water until tender. Drain. Place in baking dish. Cook pepper and onion in butter until tender. Blend in flour, salt and pepper. Add milk and cook until thick stirring constantly. Pour over cabbage and cook at 375 for 20 minutes. Combine mayonnaise, cheese and chili sauce and pour over cabbage. Bake 5 additional minutes or until cheese is melted

Snap Beans with Red Potatoes

3	lbs	fresh snap beans			salt and black pepper to taste
1	lb	fresh red potatoes	4	tbl	oil
		smoked neckbone or ham hock			

Remove tips from beans and snap. Wash to remove dirt. Wash potatoes to remove dirt and cut into halves or fourths depending on size. Place beans and potatoes in boiler and add neckbone. Salt and pepper to taste. Add water to cover beans and then add oil. Boil until beans are tender

Squash Casserole

2	lbs	squash		1	cup	sharp cheddar cheese grated
1	med	onion chopped		2	tbl	butter
1	jar	pimento, chopped		2	tsp	salt
2		eggs beaten		1	can	cream of chicken soup

Cook squash until tender. Drain and mash. Add remaining ingredients and stir. Pour into greased dish and bake for 25 to 30 minutes at 350°. Top with more grated cheese and return to oven to melt

Squash Dressing

2	cups	yellow squash diced		1	can	cream of chicken soup
1	med	onion chopped		¼	cup	butter melted
1	cup	water				salt and black pepper to taste
2	cups	cornbread crumbs		1	cup	cheddar cheese, grated
2		eggs				

Combine squash, onion and water in sauce pan. Cover and cook until tender. Drain and mash. Combine with remaining ingredients except cheese and spoon into greased casserole dish. Top with cheese and bake at 350° for 25 minutes or until thoroughly heated.

Super Taters

5 to 6	lg	potatoes, peeled and sliced	1	can	milk
		salt and black pepper to taste	1	tbl	paprika
1		can cream of chicken soup			

Peel and slice potatoes and put in a greased baking dish. Mix soup, milk, salt pepper and paprika and pour over lightly salted potatoes. Cover and bake at 425° until tender

Sweet Potato Casserole

2	cups	sweet potatoes boiled and mashed	**Topping**		
1	cup	milk	¾	cup	corn flakes crushed
2		eggs beaten	½	cup	brown sugar
1	cup	sugar	½	cup	pecans, chopped
½	tsp	nutmeg	½	stick	butter (no substitutes), softened
½	tsp	cinnamon			
¾	stick	butter			

Mix casserole ingredients together and bake at 400° until brown and almost set. Mix topping ingredients together and pour over casserole. Bake for additional 10 minutes

Taters and Onions

4 to 5 lg potatoes peeled and cut into 1/2-inch cubes

1 lg onion chopped

salt and black pepper to taste

oil for frying

Peel and cube potatoes. Chop onion and add to potatoes. Add just enough oil to cover bottom of deep iron fryer. Pour in potatoes and onions then salt and pepper to taste. Fry stirring frequently until potatoes are tender. Add additional oil if needed to prevent sticking

Thickened Potatoes

3 to 4 potatoes peeled and cut into large cubes

salt and black pepper to taste

flour for thickening

Peel and cube potatoes. Boil until almost tender. Pour about 1 cup of the potato water into a bowl. Add 2 to 3 tbl flour to hot liquid and whisk to remove lumps. Once lumps have been removed and mixture is thick return to boiling potatoes. Stir constantly until mixture is thick. Add a little salt if needed

Tomato Pie

4 med tomatoes sliced

1 refrigerated pie crust

1 cup onion chopped

½ tsp salt

½ tsp pepper

2 tbl basil chopped

½ cup mayonnaise

½ cup parmesan cheese grated

½ cup cheddar cheese, grated

In deep pie dish, bake pie crust according to package directions. Preheat oven to 375°. Cut 6 tomato slices for garnish and set aside. Halve remaining tomatoes and remove seeds. Cut each half into 4-6 wedges. Place half of the tomato wedges in the bottom of the baked pie shell. Sprinkle with half of the onion, salt, pepper and basil. Stir mayonnaise, parmesan and cheddar together in small bowl. Then spread half of the mixture over the onion layer. Repeat using remaining ingredients to create second layer. Set reserved tomato slices on top of pie. Bake 30-40 minutes until golden brown. Cover edges of pie crust with aluminum foil if pie begins to over brown. Allow pie to cool 20 minutes before serving. For best results, slice with serrated knife.

Turnip Greens

2 bundles turnips

smoked neckbone or ham hock

salt to taste

¼ cup oil

turnip roots

Take a large bundle of fresh turnips with roots. Remove stems and heavy vein from each leaf. Peel roots and cut into large cubes and set aside. Wash turnips in cold water until all grit and dirt is gone. I wash them about 8 times or until I do not feel any residue in the bottom of the sink. Place greens in a large pot and add a hunk of smoked neckbone. Fill to top of greens with water. Add salt, ¼ cup oil and peeled and cubed roots. Boil until tender. After cooking, dip greens into a bowl and crisscross 2 knives to cut. Save juice and add cut up onions to make "pot likker"

Vidalia Onion Casserole

4	cups	vidalia onions, chopped	2	cups	milk
1	stick	butter	1	cup	sharp cheddar cheese grated
20		saltines crusded			salt and black pepper to taste
4		eggs beaten			

Saute onions in ½ stick butter. Mix crushed saltines with ½ stick butter. Place cracker mixture in bottom of casserole dish. Add onions on top of crackers. Mix eggs, milk, cheese and salt. Pour over onions. Bake at 350° until set

Index

7557706R0

Made in the USA
Charleston, SC
17 March 2011